Cross–Country Skiing Today

Cross–Country Skiing
Today ✲✲ John Caldwell

THE STEPHEN GREENE PRESS   BRATTLEBORO, VERMONT

AUTHOR'S ACKNOWLEDGMENT

The generosity of the following people and organizations was prompted by their feeling for cross-country skiing, and I thank them.

None of the skiers whose pictures appear in this book asked for or received any remuneration, gift or benefit for giving permission to be photographed.

Grateful acknowledgment also is made to Tim Caldwell for photographs 24–44, 51–64 and 70–84; to the Eastern Ski Association for Nos. 91, 92, 93 and 95; John Fish for 86; Richard L. Harris for 21; Geordie Heller for 3, 4, 5, 6, 8, 102, 103 and 106; Jarl Omholt–Jensen for 113; Larry McDonald for 22; NPT Telefoto, Austria, for 23; Russ Schleipman for 87; Ski for Light, Inc., for 88; Mrs. Ethel Smalley for 20; the Swedish Information Service for No. 1; Andras Szelenyi for 19; Woodcrest Corporation, North Bradford, N.H., for 115. Norman Rogers drew No. 7. The remaining photographs are mine.

SKIPERSONS

Let me set down the gender word-combinations *he/she, his/hers, him/her* once and for all right now, because it's the last time you'll see them in this book.

No slight intended: I applaud women's increasing participation in all activities formerly considered men's-only domain. It's just a matter of how I have always written, and I find it very awkward to haul up short and insert "or she," etc., as though I were one of those writers who pointedly follow such usage these days. Therefore "he" is used in the general, and pretty obvious, way hereafter. And "chairman" means the person in charge, whether male or—sorry: whether female or male.—J. C.

This book has been produced in the United States of America, and is designed by R. L. Dothard Associates. It is published by The Stephen Greene Press, Brattleboro, Vermont 05301.

LIBRARY OF CONGRESS CATALOGING IN PUBLICATION DATA

Caldwell, John H   1928–
    Cross-country skiing today.
    Includes index.
    1. Cross-country skiing—United States.
    2. Cross-country skiing—Canada.
    I. Title
GV854.9.C7C33   796.9'3   77-79288
ISBN 0-8289-0315-8
ISBN 0-8289-0316-6 pbk.

PUBLISHED OCTOBER 1977
Second printing November 1977
Third printing July 1978
Fourth printing September 1978

Contents

1: The X–C Revolution

Who could have foretold, nearly a decade and a half ago, that cross-country skiing would achieve the popularity in North America that it enjoys today? Not me, frankly—even though I felt strongly enough about "x–c" to write a book to introduce to the general public the joys and satisfactions of this oldest of snow sports.

Of course back in the early 1960's there were people engaged in cross-country skiing, but they were relatively few. Some were

1. From a helicopter, one view of x–c: start of the Big One—the 85–km Vasaloppet in Sweden.

athletes on high school and college teams, many of whom competed in order to make theirs a four-event team by adding x–c to downhill, slalom and jumping. Then there were also a few hikers, chubbers and backpackers who wanted to get out during the winter, and preferred x–c to snowshoeing. And then there were some just plain old x–c skiers; but not many, really.

Equipment in the '60's was not readily available either, so I described the method for cutting down wooden—yes, wooden—Alpine skis in order to have something to x–c on. I described x–c waxing in the simplest terms, trying to attract a crowd, as they say. And so on. That old book is practically a collector's item now. I get great fun reading through it; and, since I'm an uncomplicated soul, there's a good deal of rueful nostalgia for those simpler days, because things have changed so fast I feel that it could have been written a hundred years ago.

During the '60's interest in x–c grew steadily and rather rapidly. Many observers attributed this to the increased leisure time enjoyed by most North Americans, some ascribed it to increased interest in physical fitness. And there were those who claimed that many Alpine skiers had become disenchanted with long lift-lines and expense, and switched to cross-country. I think this last notion has been overplayed. There's nothing against Alpine skiing, especially on those days when you hit it just right. The same can be said of x–c skiing. X–C can stand on its own merits and doesn't really need the claim of having attracted dissidents from any other sport. But it's plain and clear to me what has happened: More and more people are discovering that x–c is a good thing and are taking it up.

The growth in x–c prompted a completely rewritten treatment in 1971. Many skiers wanted more information on waxing, where to ski, how to organize tour races, what to do in planning a one-day tour off the beaten track, and so on. However, there were not many technical changes in the sport through the early '70's. Racers and tourskiers used the same techniques in skiing, the same equipment, the same waxing methods, pretty much the same clothing. The only differences were ones of degree, and I continually used racers as references in describing something for the tourskier. This same approach remained valid through the next two versions.

SO WHY A NEW BOOK?

Now we come to this book, and the natural question is: How come? Is there a need for this one?

My answer is an emphatic Yes. The mid–'70's will probably go down in North American x–c skiing as the period of the great changes, the revolution even, which I can encapsulate with two references to the racing scene. Although I think you will see the influence that racing has had on touring, when you finish reading this chapter I hope you will realize the important differences that now exist between racing and touring. And I hope that you will not fall prey to getting hooked on the racing scene—unless you're a racer, of course.

NO. 1: MAGNUSSON'S SKIS

At the 1974 World Ski Championships—the FIS (Fédération Internationale de Ski) events—a Swede named Thomas Magnusson used fiberglass racing skis in winning the first one, the men's 30-kilometer race. With one stroke his performance made certain the pending switch from wood to fiberglass racing skis. Later during the FIS the men's 15-km was won on wood skis, but this was not enough to stem the tide. The main reason more medals were not won on fiberglass skis in 1974 is that the new skis were not available to all racers; yet during the prestigious Holmenkollen meet about one month later, nearly all the top skiers were experimenting with fiberglass. Two years later, at the 1976 Olympic Games in Seefeld, not one skier I know of used wood skis in any race.

In the short period of less than two racing seasons, wood skis, which had been used in races forever, disappeared. The touring industry is following suit now.

NO. 2: KOCH'S SILVER MEDAL

It was at Seefeld in 1976 that the other breakthrough occurred, and, coincidentally, that too took place in the first x–c event, the men's 30–km. Bill Koch placed second and became the first North American to win an x–c medal in Olympic competition. His performance and its coverage by the TV networks and the newspapers around the United States and Canada helped to introduce x–c to the general public.

In sum, the switch from wood to fiberglass has created major technical changes, and Koch's performance has created a new surge of interest in the sport.

How the Skis Work for the Racer

To help understand the important technical changes occurring in x–c I'll begin by describing some of the characteristics of the new racing skis.

First of all, the new fiberglass skis are narrower than any skis made heretofore. They are best suited for use in well-prepared tracks: you shouldn't expect to have good luck going out for a tour in deep snow with them.

Next, the skis are designed so as not to turn easily, because racers don't turn much. They just go as straight and as fast as possible.

Third, since the ski bottoms are fiberglass they are much faster, or more slippery, than wood.

Last and most important, though, is the flex pattern that is built into these racing skis. In general, they are quite stiff in their mid-section, and it takes a strong skier to flatten them against the snow in order to "set" his wax—that is, to make the wax hold, or "work." Perhaps you can see the advantages to racers here. They are interested in speed. The wax usually applied under the mid-section of the ski is slower than the wax applied to the tips and tails; therefore if that slower wax does not easily come in contact with the snow—except when the racer wants it to, as in climbing a hill—his skis will be faster.

To look at it another way: When the racer stands evenly on both skis the wax under the foot is not in firm contact with the snow. But the wax on the tips and tails *is*. Then when the skier is gliding on both skis he is riding more on the fast wax, and is therefore faster.

How does this affect the tourskier? Well, most tourskiers are simply not strong enough to use fiberglass racing skis. Not being in the racer's top physical condition, the tourskier cannot continually apply enough downward force on the skis in order to set the wax. So the tourer slips a lot when using fiberglass racing skis.

But I'm getting ahead of myself.

DIFFERENT WAXING

Most skis being made for touring these days are also of fiberglass, and require care and waxing a lot different from what we used with wood ones. In addition, there are many new so-called waxless skis on the market which are causing quite a sensation. Therefore the chapters on Equipment and on Care of Equipment have both been drastically changed, nearly totally rewritten, for this book.

If you know something about the waxing of skis you will have already inferred that waxing methods are changing with the advent of fiberglass. Not only that: with the waxless skis there is a minimum need for waxing. And so the chapter on Waxing has been rewritten to take care of the changes here.

Further, since so many more skiers today are knowledgeable about waxing, I have taken a different approach to this art. And, primarily for the eager beaver, some very sophisticated waxing methods are also covered.

DIFFERENT TECHNIQUES

Because of the new skis, a new racing technique is evolving. Racers are training harder and getting stronger every year. The stronger they are the more able they are to use a fairly stiff fiberglass ski, and literally slam it down into the snow in order to set the wax which gives them hold, or purchase, from slipping back. To do this requires more of a herky-jerky motion than was needed with the more limber wood ski, and if you watch some racers you will begin to notice this.

This new racing technique is not advised for tourskiers. Stay away from it. You can best achieve the same effect by getting skis which are the right flex for you (see the Equipment chapter) and by learning to ski "the old way." Given the right skis, the old way is still the most efficient, and I'll continue to use it, even when I'm racing in veterans' events.

Just to sort of thumb my nose at this new racing style as applied to the tourskier, I have rewritten much of the Technique chapter, taking a brand new approach to learning the diagonal. I can tell you now that it may not work with racing skis—and if this disappoints you, you'd better throw this book away right now.

In a Nutshell

If I could summarize the important changes in one sentence (and this could easily be called an oversimplification) it would go like this: Between the new racing skis and the new waxing methods for them, a new racing technique has evolved.

Tourskiers are advised to stay off the new racing skis and to forget about the new racing technique. This book does not go into great detail on either the new fiberglass racing skis or the new technique they call for.

However, as in the past, I will make occasional references to the racing scene and I do this to add color. My comments will also underline the great difference that now exists between racing and recreational skiing.

With the advent of the new skis and the technique they entail, today cross-country skiing could be called a sport of contrasts. There are so many different ways to ski, so many places to ski, so many different conditions one can ski in, so many different kinds of equipment. On and on. I take a good example from the equipment line. It's still possible to get a complete x–c outfit—this includes skis, poles, boots and bindings—for around $85.00. On the other hand, many a racer these days is using new super-light, carbonfiber poles. Their price? Around $85.00.

IT'S YOUR OWN THING

All of which brings me to my over-all feeling about x–c. It's my main pitch and hasn't changed.

Cross-country skiing should be fun for everyone. The range of possibilities for enjoyment is unlimited. You can ski anywhere there's snow, you can use a wide variety of equipment, you can ski alone or with a group, you can use the very best technique while wearing the clothes you just picked up from the local rummage sale, or you can wear the latest styles and invent your own technique. So pick out and use anything you want from this book —but most of all, have fun skiing x–c. Make it be your thing.

NO WORD GAMES

Just two more points.

First, I use "cross-country skiing," "ski touring" and "running" interchangeably throughout. Some people insist that the phrase "cross-country skiing" means something very rugged, or something nearly approaching racing. To me, x–c skiing means skiing across the countryside: a simple, literal translation. In the comparatively few places where I think it more helpful to differentiate between x–c casual skiing and x–c racing I will just flag the sections which refer to racing.

2. And another aspect: alone in the quiet of winter.

Next, this is not a book on ski-mountaineering. The business of overnight trips, coping in avalanche country, special equipment (including skins put under skis for climb), packs and cooking utensils are highly specialized things which I am not going to treat. I am not an expert on these matters, and they are well covered in mountaineering publications such as those of the Sierra Club, and *Wilderness Camping* and *Mountain Gazette*.

As I predicted a few years ago, there has been a proliferation of ski-touring areas around the country. Now you can go to several touring centers and begin the sport from scratch, just as you might do for Alpine skiing.

There is more attention being paid to x–c. I never dreamed I would see the gear advertised on TV—the newspapers yes, but the *tube!* There are more experts in the field. There are more and more professional touring instructors. And last, there are more and more books on the subject.

Well, here's the completely up-to-date sequel to the original. Good reading to you.

2: Equipment

As more and more new, fairly sophisticated x–c equipment appears on the market you will hear arguments for various ski constructions, different materials, different lengths, widths, flexes, and so on. It can be mind-boggling. Still, though, there are a few things we can be fairly sure of during the next few years, and before I describe the present equipment scene, I list these tenets:

1. *It's safe to say that equipment manufacturers are out to make money,* and therefore you can expect them to exert pressures, however subtle, to get you to buy new equipment every season or two.

2. *New equipment will continue to appear each year.* But if your present equipment works well, stick with it until it wears out—unless *you* want to change. Remember, this is your sport and you do it the way you want to.

3. *Wood skis are definitely on the way out.* The x–c industry is following the pattern established by the Alpine people several years ago. I began my skiing career on wood Alpine skis. I even started x–c on Alpine ski cut-downs, those marvelous exhibits with the sections containing the steel edges trimmed off to make a narrow, at that time sleek-looking, x–c ski. I haven't seen any wood Alpine skis for a long time and the wood x–c skis are fast disappearing.

4. *Shy away from racing skis unless you are a competitor.* Most good racing skis being produced these days can be described as having what the auto manufacturers call high performance characteristics. That is, the skis are very light and narrow, suited best for skiing in well-prepared, hard tracks. The flex built into the skis is such that only strong, well-conditioned athletes can make the skis work, or set the wax.

You might wax a pair of these racing skis with klister and use them successfully for a kilometer or two. But unless you are in good shape, the force needed to set the wax with every stride will soon tire you out. And as soon as you get tired your skis will begin to slip. Then you'll think you have the wrong wax.

14

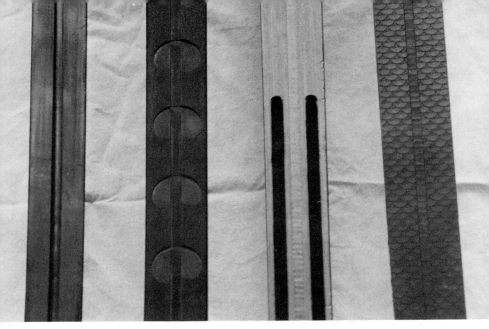

3. Fiberglass ski bottoms. From left to right: a waxable racing ski; a light waxless touring ski with one version of the fishscale principle; a light waxless touring ski with mohair strips; a waxless touring ski with fishscale bottom.

Not so. You simply have the wrong skis. They are too stiff for you.

5. *If you need some new equipment, take the time to test different types.* There are plenty of skis available these days and you can rent them at x–c ski areas, or shops that specialize in x–c. Or you can go out with a friend who has a spare pair and make some tests and comparisons. Look into it to find what suits you best.

The Skis

In getting new equipment your most important decision will be in choosing between waxable and waxless skis.

WAXABLE, OR WAXLESS?

Waxable skis require—well—waxing. They are the traditional ones, for most people who know x–c.

If you are a good waxer, or if you enjoy waxing, or if you want to learn about waxing, you will probably be happier with waxable skis. Compared to waxless skis, most of the time you can get better skiing with waxable skis because well-waxed skis are generally faster and climb more efficiently than their waxless counterparts do.

But the ski manufacturers are working very hard at perfecting new models of waxless skis; perhaps in the near future they will come up with something that even beats the waxable type. Meanwhile, there is a burden on the manufacturers of ski wax to produce some better, more universal waxes. Here is a situation where the competition in business is benefiting everyone.

The disadvantages of waxable skis should be clear: They require waxing, perhaps every time you go skiing. The process takes time and the wax costs money. In addition, waxing is something of an art and not everyone can master its details (see the chapter on Waxing).

THE CHALLENGE OF WAXABLES

I enjoy waxing x–c skis as much as anyone around. I began fooling around with wax in the 1940's and probably will keep at it until I quit skiing. I feel that waxing is a part of the sport, that it adds to the challenges. Cross-country wouldn't be the same to me without it.

O.K., maybe I'm prejudiced. I especially love to wax and go out for a spin around my Vermont neighborhood to see if I can get through all the various snow conditions without having my ski bottoms ice up. In the spring, waxing often poses a problem because the south slopes are warmed and the north slopes may still be powdery. I go ahead and wax anyway, enjoying that expectancy or suspense while I wonder how my wax will work. Some places I am forced to use slightly different techniques, being careful not to lift the skis; in other sections I might have to stomp the skis down hard in order to set the wax. But if I hit the wax right, and make these adjustments in technique, I can ski happily in most of the terrain.

That isn't the only fun part of waxing for me. When I come home I usually clean the wax off in preparation for another day. This ritual takes the place of a warm-down after the tour; and I communicate with my skis, just the way Mark Fidrych talks to the baseballs when he is pitching.

Waxable skis basically come in two materials—wood and fiber-glass. Some fiberglass skis are made entirely of synthetic materials and some have bits and pieces of wood in them. The importance of the fiberglass or other synthetics in a ski is this: Fiberglass makes the skis stronger and less breakable; the fiberglass, or synthetic, bottom surface is stronger, tougher, faster, and more water-resistant than wood; the synthetic materials allow a more uniform—even a programmed—method of construction. Top racers tell the factories exactly how stiff they want their skis under the foot, just ahead of the foot, in the tip, and so on. And they get them that way.

Much as I have used wood x–c skis, and lovely as they are, to-day I must—shedding a tear or two—vote for the synthetic-ma-terials construction.

THE WAXLESS ONES

Waxless skis are those that don't require waxing in order to get purchase, or climb, for skiing x–c. The main reason for having a waxless ski is to get grip without having to wax. This means that you can go skiing regularly without going through the folderol of waxing.

The speed of the waxless ski is a secondary consideration right now. It has to be, mainly because the manufacturers haven't come up with a really fast waxless ski and therefore cannot make claims in this area. So make no mistake about it, you sacrifice some speed with waxless skis. Nevertheless most users of waxless skis are willing to give this up. In fact, I know lots of tourskiers who like their skis a bit slow on the downhill.

All waxless skis are made basically with synthetic materials, although some contain wood in their innards. However, your choice isn't between wood and synthetic here, but instead is a matter of opting for a particular bottom—and I'll get to these in just a minute.

Waxless skis are great, and they are providing thrills for many newcomers to the sport. There is just one basic drawback to them, and it's a mechanical sort of thing. Waxless skis cannot change to accommodate snow conditions. They are the same every time you go skiing, no matter what sort of snow you have underfoot. With waxable skis, as you may know, the wax can be made different every time you go skiing, and therefore your skis are made more effective for the snow conditions.

Mohair and Its Variations

In broad terms, there are two different bottom surfaces on waxless skis. Some manufacturers might insist that their brand deserves a special category, but I'll stick with my arbitrary two in order to keep things simple at this stage. A more detailed breakdown will be noted in "Technical Points in Choosing a Ski," listed soon.

The first type of waxless ski has so-called mohair strips; "so-called" because some of the strips are not actually mohair, but they do serve the same purpose. In the mohair type there are two subdivisions: one having a mohair strip on each side of the groove, the other having a single broader strip that spans the width of the ski.

For the purpose of this discussion, the other main waxless category embraces all non-mohair bottoms, where special configurations are provided on the actual surface.

In the 1976 Winter Olympics at Seefeld, 30–km silver medalist Bill Koch used skis with mohair while running the third leg of the 4 x 10 relay race. The conditions were ideal for mohair. The tracks in the stadium at the start were very glazed, the temperature was near freezing, but as the course reached the higher northern slopes the snow was much drier. Many skiers using conventional fiberglass racing skis and conventional wax—whatever "conventional wax" could be for these conditions!—iced up on the course and had to stop and de-ice before finishing. Koch had an outstanding time on his leg and thereby really put mohair skis on the map.

It's important to note, though, that he used waxable skis in his other races—including the 30–km event—and so did everyone else. The result has been that, however much most racers shun the use of waxless skis these days, you will find a pair or two in their ski bags for possible use when snow conditions like those just mentioned defy most waxing jobs.

As a note of interest I mention that the U.S. Ski Team pioneered the research of all kinds of waxless skis for racing. Koch's

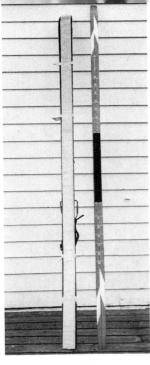

4. Left, an Alpine ski with the fine old-style skins for climbing (especially in ski mountaineering); right, the fairly short kicker zone of this x–c racing ski has a solid mohair strip.

use of these skis was no accident. Here is a situation where the U.S. skiers are setting trends for the rest of the world in x-c. Maybe the Russians, or perhaps some Scandinavians, will soon report that they discovered these waxless skis for racing, but I'm telling you 't ain't so.

How Mohair Works

The mohair strips are laid in the bottom with the hairs lying in the direction of tip to tail. When you press the ski down in the snow these little hairs grip, or dig into the snow, to prevent the ski from slipping back. When you slide the ski forward the hairs lie flat and do not present so much friction—although there is some, depending on the size of the strips.

The mohair principle is nothing new to Alpine skiers who took a leaf from the ski-mountaineering buffs' book and used skins to climb mountains during the 1930's, '40's, and early '50's before so many ski lifts were built. I remember climbing the Wildcat trail at Pinkham Notch, New Hampshire, many times, just to get up there to be able to race back down. The skins we used extended the full length of our Alpine skis and we could climb anything.

Our team manager always came along with an empty rucksack and carried the skins back down the trail for us. Some other teams were not so lucky, though, and many a racer had to wrap the skins around his waist and race with them. Can you imagine present-day Alpine racers schussing the slopes with all those straps dangling about, causing all that restriction and wind resistance? No way!

Machined Bottoms, and How They Work

The other general waxless ski contains steps, many small ridges, diamonds or some other configuration on the bottom surface. These features help the ski from slipping back when it is pressed into the snow, and they are an integral part of the bottom surface. (The technical-minded people in the industry have further classified these bottoms as being "positive-base" or "negative-base" skis according to whether the steps, etc., protrude from the bottom or are incised in the bottom.)

The most notable variety in this category is the fishscale bottom. Made to resemble overlapping discs, this was the first construction used in manufacturing waxless skis. Today it is probably found on more waxless skis than any other bottom.

It is interesting that the fishscale construction was originally used on Alpine skis in an effort to make them faster. I know that some of the skiers testing these fishscale models were amazed at how well they could ski on them—*uphill*. The idea was sold and patented and now the fishscale is used solely on x–c skis. The other designs, such as diamonds, ridges, steps, etc., are used by different companies who do not hold the fishscale patent.

TECHNICAL POINTS IN CHOOSING A SKI

The many different types of waxless skis present, to me, a certain irony. For, the minute anyone begins to study all the waxless skis and the variables that affect their performance, the subject can get as complicated, or more so, than waxing. And the idea of waxless skis is to have something simple that works without waxing, right?

Well, you don't really have to know how the waxless skis work, but it is interesting that many of the theories behind them also apply to waxing. If you ask yourself the questions I list below it might help you to pick out a pair of waxless skis that is well suited to you—and you'll have the beginnings of some waxing theory too.

How long should the strips be? Should there be two strips?—or just one, full width? Clearly, the longer and wider the strips, the more purchase you will get, but at the sacrifice of some speed.

Where should the strips be located with respect to the middle of the ski? Should they be centered on the mid-point, forward of it, or behind it? The answer to this is complicated and depends on how you ski, how strong you are, what the flex of your skis is, etc.

How deeply into the bottom should the strips be laid? The farther in, the less grip; the farther out, the more grip and friction.

IN CONSIDERING MACHINED BOTTOMS

How close together should the steps, etc., be? The more steps, the more ridges to hold against slipping—but the more friction too.

ICING PROBLEMS

Some of the mohair strips ice up, especially when you ski from wet snow or slush into powder. You can easily see how this happens: The mohair picks up the water in the track and then ices when it comes in contact with colder, drier snow. If you are very careful to keep your skis on the snow surface and not lift them when you go through these different conditions, this will help. But you may still ice up.

Another method used by many skiers and touring centers to prevent icing is to lubricate the strips with silicone spray, or some equivalent. This helps.

The step-type bottoms often do not work well on very hard-packed or icy conditions. You can imagine the skis' slipping back more easily if the snow or the track is not soft enough for the skis to indent, or make an imprint.

How deep should the steps be? The deeper they are the more hold you will get. But again, deep steps will cause the skis to be slower on the flats and downhills.

Should the steps be positive—that is, protruding from the running surface of the ski? Or negative—that is, incised into the running surface? Generally, the positive steps grip better, but are also slower, than the negative designs.

Should the cuts or steps be graduated so they are deeper under the foot where more force is exerted, and shallower fore and aft of this section?

How much of the running surface should the steps cover?

The answers to all these questions depend on the flex of the ski, the depth of the cuts, the way you ski, and so on.

In most cases you won't have much to do with determining how the manufacturers build their skis, but you can be sure that they are continually experimenting with different types. I expect they soon will have models with different characteristics for different people and different snow conditions.

HOW EASY TO REPAIR?

One important factor in choosing a waxless ski is its "repairability." If you use your skis enough, and if snow conditions are very harsh, the bottoms will wear out and need replacing. Some bottoms are more easily replaced than others. For instance, you can buy mohair strips for some skis and put them in yourself. For the skis with non-mohair bottoms, a few companies service their products; others do not.

You would be best off buying a pair of skis which can be repaired by you, your shop, or by the company. So look into it. Ask when you make your purchase.

FOR BEGINNER, INTERMEDIATE, EXPERT

I highly recommend waxless skis for beginners. However, I cannot recommend one variety over another. If you are just starting you have the opportunity to try different models. Visit a touring area and rent some equipment. Check with friends to see if they have some skis you can try. Then, if you can determine which skis work best for you in the conditions prevalent in your area, go out and buy a pair.

If you are an intermediate skier who is gaining interest in x–c, and enjoys waxing, you ought to have two pairs of skis, one waxable and one waxless. Then when a situation comes up where the waxing is difficult, or you're in a hurry, you can use the waxless jobs. Other times you can wax and be well off. And there's nothing wrong with having that extra pair of skis for a friend who might go out with you.

For experts, again I would recommend having two pairs of skis, one waxless and one waxable. I think, though, that you'll use the waxless skis only when the waxing conditions are extremely difficult. For the present and until the waxless skis are much improved, you will get the best ride on a well-waxed ski. If you are in a hurry to go skiing you will have to decide whether you want to take the time to wax and have a good ski, or not wax and have a bit more time to ski on waxless skis—but at a different speed, or pace.

SKI LENGTHS

The old reliable standard still holds: To measure the ski length correct for you, stand on the floor and reach up with your hand. The tip of the ski should come to your wrist.

If you are light for your height, you can go either of two ways in picking out a pair of skis. One is to look for a ski that is relatively soft, or flexible. The other is to get a ski that is slightly shorter; for example, if you measure for a 205–centimeter length, get a 200–cm ski.

It then follows that if you are heavy for your height you should look for a stiffer pair of skis. This is preferable to getting a slightly longer pair, although you might have to go for the extra length in order to get the correct flex.

TESTS FOR FLEXIBILITY

With so many different kinds of waxable and waxless skis on the market it is important, and possible, to find some that are the right flex for you. Having the right flex means that the skis will work well. When you wax them correctly you will be able to set the wax, get good purchase, and use good technique to motor along the flats and uphills. And when you use the waxless skis you will be able to get good purchase with them.

If the skis are too stiff you are likely to have difficulty and slip more than you should.

Don't be led astray by judging the skis' camber alone. While camber and flexibility are somewhat related, testing only for camber will not be a guarantee that your skis are the right flex. Here are three simple tests that will help you:

1. *You can give the skis the squeeze test.* Hold them, bottoms facing, and squeeze. Simple!—they should come together evenly the entire length, with the tips separating a little. Now grab another pair and squeeze them. If you test enough skis you will notice that some are softer than others.

In general, if you have a ski the right length, you need a slightly more soft (i.e., flexible) ski if you are light for your height, and a slightly stiffer ski if you are, shall I say, rugged for your height.

2. *You can use the paper-sliding test.* Put the skis on a smooth, hard floor; stand on them and have a friend try slipping a piece of paper under them where your feet are. If the paper slides between the floor and the skis comfortably, these skis are right for you. If the paper doesn't slide under, the skis are too soft. If there is a big gap and you could slide several pieces of paper underneath (or a piece of cardboard), the skis are too stiff.

Many racers put marks on the sides of their skis to show how far the paper has slid fore and aft. This area is called the kicker zone, and is used as a guide in applying purchase waxes (which are discussed in the Waxing chapter).

With mohair strips there will be some impediments, especially when you try to slide the paper forward, against the grain of the hairs. You'll have to be careful testing these skis.

3. *Check the bottoms of waxable skis after a trial tour.* If the wax is worn evenly, the skis are the right flex for you. If the wax is worn off the tips and tails, the skis are too stiff. If the wax is worn off under the foot, the skis are too soft, or limber.

With waxless skis you can check them as you ski. If you get pretty good purchase on the flats and fairly good purchase on the uphills you certainly have some skis that are working. If the skis do slip it might be because of the conditions, so don't despair. Take the skis out another day, in different snow conditions, and see if they work better.

Of the extremes, it's better to have a ski that is too limber. At

Equipment

least this way you can use the wax under the foot—where it's very important—until it wears off. Or, the waxless section of your ski—which is located primarily under the foot—will grab for you.

SKI WIDTHS

Most x–c skis are wider at tip and tail than at the waist. If you want to be exact and measure x–c skis for width at their tips and tails as well as right under the waist at the binding point, you will come up with at least a hundred different combinations. For purposes of simplification I group skis in three different categories, according to the width under the binding at the narrowest part of the ski. Touring skis are about 55 millimeters (2 1/16 inches) wide; light touring skis, about 48–51 mm (just less than 2 inches); racing skis, about 45–47 mm (well under 2 inches). Each ski has its special advantages.

FOR THE TOURING SKI

Tourers are slightly wider than most x–c skis and therefore heavier, a bit stiffer, more rugged and less wobbly. They usually weigh between 2,000 to 2,500 grams, or in the 5-to-6-pound category. Many beginners prefer these skis because they provide more stability and are easier to learn the sport on. Often the deep-powder addict in the western part of North America used to get these wider skis because they didn't sink as deep into the snow as the narrower versions do. But now some companies have come out with special skis for deep powder and these measure as wide as 81 mm (3 1/4 inches) at the waist. So if your bag is a lot of deep-powder skiing, get hold of these skis.

FOR THE LIGHT TOURING SKI

The light touring ski is enough narrower, lighter and more flexible to feel like a racing ski compared with the touring skis described above. They weigh between 1,500 and 2,200 grams (3 1/2 to 5 pounds), and generally the fiberglass skis are lighter than wood skis of the same width.

Don't be scared off by my racing comparison. This is the ski I would recommend for most skiers, even beginners. Lots of people I know have started with wide tourers only to go to narrower skis very quickly after discovering how easy x–c skiing is. Anyway, the trend is definitely toward lighter equipment. Tracks and trails are better every year, and can accommodate the narrower skis. Skiers' abilities, too, are improving; and in a sport where much emphasis is on freedom of movement and lightness of equipment, these are the skis that make the most sense for the most people.

I even know a few tourskiers who have racing skis on hand as spares, or just in case they happen to want to enter a little race some day.

FOR THE RACING SKI

The racing ski is super-light, narrower and more fragile than the others. Mine weigh less than 3 pounds, and some carbonfiber skis weigh only about 1,000 grams (slightly over 2 pounds). These skis are designed specifically for racing on fast, well-prepared tracks, and if you try them and have difficulties with them breaking or delaminating on you, or being hard to turn (having little or no side camber as mentioned below), you have no one to blame but yourself.

Racing skis have undergone more radical changes in design

NOT FAR, NOT WIDE

Many Alpine skiing instructors have been using a system called the Graduated Length Method to teach beginning skiers. It works very well: Beginners start with very short skis, learn how to handle them, then graduate to longer skis, and so on.

This approach has been tried in x–c, but most instructors agree that it isn't necessary since the x–c ski length, assuming it is correct, does not really pose a problem to the beginning skier. But some instructors thought it might be a good idea to try a graduated-*width* method wherein beginners start on relatively wide skis, then graduate to narrower skis as they improve their balance. However, this approach has not swept through the ranks of x–c ski schools because, I suspect, for most people there isn't a pronounced difference between, say, a ski of touring width and one of light-touring width.

than any others, and this trend is likely to continue. For a while some racing skis had no side camber—that is, unlike the various tourers, their width measurements were the same at the tip, the waist and the tail. This made the racing skis difficult to turn, but the theory was that the tracks were so well set that the racers wouldn't need the conventional design. At about the same time, though, the race courses became more challenging, often having what I call screaming, or fast, downhill sections with turns. Many racers couldn't hang on to these turns, partly because of their skis, which did not turn easily. At this writing, there is a trend toward a small amount of side camber in racing skis. But all this is just another reason to stay away from racing skis unless you are a serious competitor.

Summarizing: The wider the ski is, the more it weighs. Fiberglass skis are usually lighter and more rugged than their wood counterparts. Racing skis are usually much lighter, more fragile, and harder to turn than touring or light touring skis. You can get a wide range of light touring skis, and most skiers are advised to stick with this category.

The Poles

The pole situation is not so complicated as the ski picture. You have a good choice here and usually get what you pay for.

The lightest, and most expensive, poles being made these days are used for racing. They utilize carbonfiber construction, weigh a mere 70 grams—about 2 1/2 ounces!—and cost around $85.00. These are not recommended for most skiers, for reasons I will cite below.

You can get poles made of fiberglass, metal or tonkin (bamboo). It's worth your time to get metal or fiberglass because they will not break so easily as tonkin. And tonkin poles may go off the market soon anyway.

General Checklist

There are some things to watch for in choosing an all-purpose x–c pole:

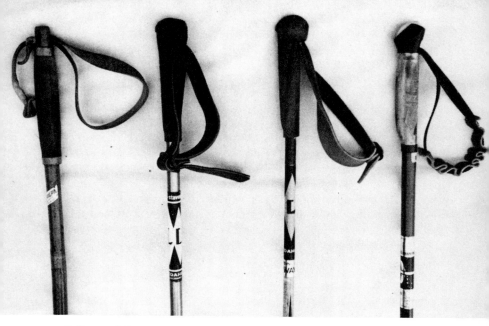

5. Some of the various styles of grips and straps for x–c poles.

1. *Get your poles the right height.* Stand on the floor, and the poles should fit comfortably under your armpits.

2. *Be sure the pole tip is curved forward* so that it pulls out of the snow when you ski. Don't get stuck with a straight-tipped Alpine pole, which will hang up in the snow as your ski slides by it.

3. If you want, here are a couple of items you can merely get fussy about. Many skiers prefer *a tight-fitting, wide strap* which offers more support when you push against it.

If you have *an adjustable strap for use in varying snow depths* it will be advantageous. By slightly loosening the strap and thereby lowering your grip on the handle, you will effectively have a shorter pole, good for use in deep tracks when the pole-track is relatively higher than normal.

Specifically Baskets

Pole baskets are of different diameters and materials. The trend is toward synthetic materials for the baskets and away from tonkin and leather.

Equipment

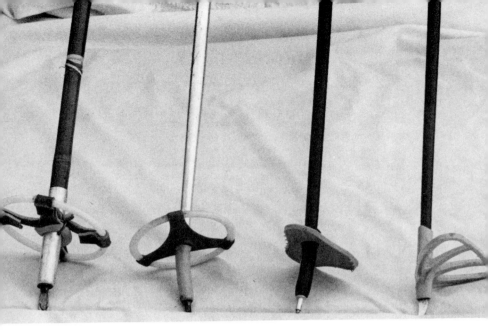

6. The developing trend in x–c poles. From left to right: traditional tonkin (bamboo) shaft, here with a plastic basket; then a metal shaft, with pole tip angled for quick withdrawal from the snow; fiberglass, with a concave basket; and carbonfiber, with a rigid basket. In 7, the drawing, note the basket in the rearmost position (it's the one second from left in the photo).

A more important trend for you is the one toward baskets of smaller diameter. The extreme in pole baskets is again illustrated by the racing side of the sport where baskets are a mere half-moon, or crescent, shape. These work well if the pole-track is packed hard. But if you try them in a soft pole-track, or in un-packed snow, the poles will be a hindrance rather than a help because they will sink in so far that you have to yank them out.

Pole Baskets   **29**

But that's not all. Many of the racing-pole baskets are an integral part of the pole; that is, they do not turn, swivel, or bend when they catch on something like a cut-off sapling. That means if you hook the basket on something it will stay there—hooked! I came a cropper one spring on my first tour with these poles when I caught a low bush on a downhill section. I was spun around right in my tracks and nearly yanked my arm out of its socket.

I've even caught these pole baskets on car bumpers as I walked through parking areas. It's kind of embarrassing to be suddenly shed of everything you're carrying in the middle of the parking lot.

I'll have to develop a new pole-carry, perhaps holding the things by the basket end when I'm in dangerous situations. But then there are those straps I can shove my feet into . . .

The Boots

You should suit your boots to your skis, which in turn should be suited to your bent and your terrain. With this in mind, you'll find the range of boots is as wide as that of skis. There are rugged models which are usually heavier and stiffer than most touring boots; these would match up with the touring skis. Then there are light touring boots and racing boots. From the touring boots you can go all the way down in lightness and flexibility to the racing boot, which weighs as little as 700 grams (about 24 ounces) a pair.

TOURING BOOTS

These boots, which approximate downhill boots in size and shape, are well designed for rugged touring or ski-mountaineering. They should have heel-grooves for use with a cable binding. They are heavier than the other models, usually stiffer, but warmer at the same time.

THE LIGHT TOURING BOOT

I would recommend the light touring boot for most skiers. There are many models on the market. You can get these in high ver-

Match the tops of new style x–c boots in Photo 8, above, with their soles below in 9. From left to right: light touring boot with leather top and sole, where holes will be drilled in the toe; then a racing boot with molded sole and pre-drilled holes; and the pioneering Adidas racer with its plastic sole extended to slide into the binding.

sions and in rather low versions. The main advantage of the higher boot is its warmth; it also keeps out the snow better. However, I don't think the higher boot gives a lot more ankle support, since the material of the sides is not that stiff.

THE RACING BOOT

This boot is literally the track shoe of the x–c world. The first breakthrough in racing boots was made by Adidas, a well-known shoe company. They simply put a special sole on a version of one of their track shoes and that was it. Now many companies are following suit.

The new racing boots are very light, very flexible, and usually very cold for the skier who doesn't move particularly fast.

These boots cannot be used in any old x–c binding, either. If you choose one company's boot you are usually forced to choose that company's binding as well.

Once again, synthetic materials have replaced the traditional leather soles. The plastics are stronger, lighter, more flexible for bending at the toes, and more stable when it comes to twisting to the side—that is, the boots give better lateral support.

The Fit

The most important thing about a boot is its fit. Be sure to try on boots with the socks you plan to wear skiing—perhaps just a pair of knicker socks, or a pair of wool socks and another, lighter pair —and then find a pair of boots that fit like street shoes.

Some boots are made on wide lasts and may not fit snugly around the heel. A loose fit here will be the cause of many blisters.

Naturally, don't get boots so short that your toes jam into the fronts of them, or else you'll lose your toenails.

If your boot has a roll of padding or some elastic material along the top around the ankle, this will help keep out the snow.

The Sole and Its Width

Almost all boots being made now have synthetic molded soles; leather is virtually gone. The new soles offer three distinct advantages. They are more waterproof than leather, their construction insures greater standardization, and the soles are pre-drilled to fit standard bindings. Some old leather-soled boots used to come through with different width soles, a drawback that made it difficult to fit them to the bindings.

The manufacturers have gone one step further and have agreed to make all their touring boots with pin toe-bindings (the most widely used tour binding, which is described below) according to the established Nordic Norm. This means that if you get such a boot from one company it will fit another company's binding. Previous to this it was often a real puzzle to find boots and bindings that matched, and it was a nightmare for coaches who had skiers with several different makes of boots. Now, chances are pretty good that you could outfit a family with interchangeable skis because the bindings would fit all the boots.

It isn't all clear sailing, though, because pin toe-bindings come in three different sizes: 71 millimeters, 75 mm and 79 mm wide, measured at the point where the pins are. But a very large percentage of the boots are made to fit the 75–mm binding width; and since the pegs in the various bindings are also compatible, it means that a narrow 71–mm boot can be used in any binding and that a 75–mm boot can be used in the two wider bindings.

The Bindings

The guys who were working hard to build better mousetraps shifted their focus to x–c bindings. I couldn't begin to describe all the different bindings that have come on the market recently. However, the move to toe-bindings is nearly complete: with the exception of mountaineers, who use cable bindings, nearly everyone uses toe-bindings.

Toe–bindings

Toe-bindings include at least four categories:

1. The traditional pin-binding usually has three strong metal pegs that stick up into the holes drilled in the sole of the boot near the toe, and a clamp (front throw) which exerts pressure downward on the sole of the boot at the toe. These bindings are simple, light, and inexpensive. We know they work; they've been used for years. Don't be afraid to stick with them in the face of pressure to use other types.

2. Another general type of toe-binding is one which holds the boot by some other means than the pins just described. I cannot describe all the variations here, but some hook into the top of the sole at the toe, others have pins that go clear through the sole of the boot at the toe; and so on. Most of these are good. Obviously, though, they can't be used interchangeably.

3. There are some step-in bindings on the market. One combination has a metal piece on the toe of the boot that interlocks with the binding on the skis as you step in. This is very convenient, but has one major drawback: the boots and bindings are not interchangeable with other, different models.

Some other step-in bindings can be hitched or unhitched by use of the ski-pole point. Perhaps you've seen some advertised showing the pole pressing down on a front-throw release. These are fine too, but I always figured that when I was skiing I was after some exercise, for one thing, and so I don't mind bending over to fasten or unfasten my bindings. (I'm also one who actually bends over to pick up tennis balls; never could master either that little bounce and pick-up with the racket, or the racket-heel lift.)

4. Finally, there are the latest racing bindings, which are suited only to boots with a special, extended sole. This extension slides snugly into a slot provided by the binding and is secured by a pin or pressure from a clamp.

There were two main reasons for making these new bindings. First, they are actually a few ounces lighter—a factor that makes a slight difference to the racers, lighter being better. Second, and probably more important, the bindings are much narrower than anything made heretofore and because they don't stick out on either side of the ski so much, they do not produce so much drag on the edge of the track. Drag is the same as friction and means slower going during a race.

Since these bindings are narrower, it means—you guessed it—that most present-day boots will not fit them. This is not really a problem for tourskiers, however, because they have no need for these super-light bindings.

There's an interesting sideline here concerning the manufacture of the new boot-and-binding combinations. Adidas came in first with their shoe and binding—I call the binding a whisper—and it received a great deal of publicity prior to and during the Winter

10. The Adidas boot-binding combo. The deeply incised "V"-notch in the heel accommodates the ridge of the heel-plate, thus providing better control on downhills.

Olympics in 1976. Not to be outdone, and in fact to go further, some other companies banded together and produced their own combinations in the form of a *new* Nordic Norm; but this is the *Racing* Norm and it's narrower than the original Norm, which is still used for most x–c equipment. Naturally the Adidas boots are not compatible with the new Norm and the racers are headed back to where they started from several years ago, when not many boot and binding items were interchangeable.

Heel–cable Bindings

Proponents of the cable binding argue that it offers some lateral support that is absent in the toe-binding. This may be true, but I feel that lateral support is primarily a function of boot construction. (Many boots with a heel-groove happen to be more rugged everywhere. If you want to make tests yourself, use a boot with a heel-groove in it, first with a cable binding and then with a toe-binding. I don't think you'll find much difference.)

Cable bindings are heavier than toe-bindings but they do offer one advantage: If you have side hitches on your skis and can loop the cable through these, you will get more downpull on your boots and therefore will be able to ski downhill more in an Alpine manner—that is, with more edging and better control of your skis. Most ski-mountaineering people use bindings of this type. When they go uphill they unhitch the cable and can lift the heel freely.

Summarizing with cautions: Be sure to get a boot that is compatible with your binding. Don't get a special step-in binding that requires a boot with a toepiece, without getting that boot, or that toepiece. Don't get wide boots and a narrow binding. And don't get one of those new racing boots with the special sole and expect it to work in your present binding.

If your boots and bindings work well, stick with 'em.

Heel–plates

You should have heel-plates on your skis, and here again there are many different shapes and materials. Made of metal, plastic, rubber or whatever, they are tacked on the ski right where the heel of your boot will fall. They keep the snow from balling up under your foot; they also offer some stability by virtue of the friction they create under your heel.

If you can't find some commercial heel-plates, use a piece of linoleum or stair-tread instead. Either will be better than nothing at all.

Some boots have a little "V" notch that fits snugly over special heel-plates. If the boots you're considering have a special groove for a heel-plate you should be sure to pick up the correct plates when you get your boots.

Note: There are further tips for youngsters' equipment in Kid Stuff, Chapter 8.

SOME RELIABLE NAMES

There's always a risk in listing sources of equipment, changes in the marketplace being what they are. Nevertheless here are some suppliers, chosen because they've been around long enough for me to assume that they will probably continue in business.

There are many other suppliers, so don't be too concerned if the one whose equipment you depend on does not appear here.

In alphabetical order, then: Adidas, Bonna, Edsbyn, Elan, Epoke, Fischer, Jarvinen, Karhu, Kneissl, Lovett, Rossignol, Ski-Lom, Splitkein, Sundins, Trak.

3: Caring for Equipment

I've always been kind of a nut about maintenance. Whether it's new skis, a lawnmower, a car or whatever, I set out to try to make the darned things last. It's easy to form a mystical association with a car through long years of use—many of us have done this. And I know plenty of people who get attached to particular skis, or boots or poles or bindings, during the lifetime of such equipment. All of them have learned the best ways to care for the stuff and try to get the most use from it. Seldom do these skiers have equipment problems and, more important to many of us, this kind of long-range approach is the most economical.

There is enough information here to serve you and your equipment well. If you take some time to work on your skis especially you'll be rewarded with better performance on the snow.

Caring for Your Skis

Let's look at the skis in three different situations: first, when they're new; next, during the season as you are using them; and, finally, when you store them for the summer.

CONDITIONING NEW SKIS

If They're Fiberglass

New fiberglass skis come with essentially two different kinds of bottoms. One is harder than the other but both are referred to often as "P–tex," or polyethylene. (I hesitate even to mention these terms since many firms have their own special-sounding, self-promoting, modern chemical-like brand names, and they like to differentiate between all the various formulas as if they were addressing the American Chemical Society, or some such group.)

FOR THE SOFTER BOTTOMS

Most people I know agree that the softer bottoms should be hot-waxed—sometimes referred to as base-waxed—before using. The best way to do this is by ironing in some Alpine soft wax (for wet snow; see the Waxing chapter for this and other terms used below). This softer wax does a better job of combining with the bottom surface than a harder wax does.

Hold the Alpine wax against the tip of a hot ordinary flatiron close to the ski and draw a trail of wax on the bottom surface on each side of the groove. Then with the iron still on the setting at *Wool* (about 140° F./60° C.), smooth the wax in. Spend some time going over the wax, since doing so insures a better job. In fact, if you hot-wax this base on several times during the season the performance of your skis will continue to improve.

After hot-waxing, scrape most of the wax off the bottom and the groove, leaving only a thin film. Metal or plastic scrapers may be used for this job, but if you use metal be sure not to scrape too hard or else you will take off some of the bottom surface as well as the wax.

Some skiers, racers especially, do not put Alpine wax on the area of the ski under the foot, where they will be applying x–c purchase (climbing) wax. This is because the x–c wax will not adhere well to the Alpine wax. So, instead, the racers use a hard x–c wax like Special Green, or a binder.

FOR HARDER BOTTOMS

Companies disagree on the preparation for fiberglass skis with the harder bottoms. Some tell you to base-wax and others tell you just to apply the wax you plan to ski on. However, no harm is done by hot-waxing and scraping as above, and I would recommend it.

If They're Wood

Most new wooden skis are sold with a coating of protective varnish or lacquer on the bottoms. This has to come off because it is deathly slow as a substitute for wax, and it doesn't even hold the wax you try to cover it with. I use a combination of strong liquid paint-remover and elbow grease—the elbow grease being needed to wield a scraper.

The most popular scraper with us is a flat rectangular steel one made by the Stanley tool company. This really has eight edges—

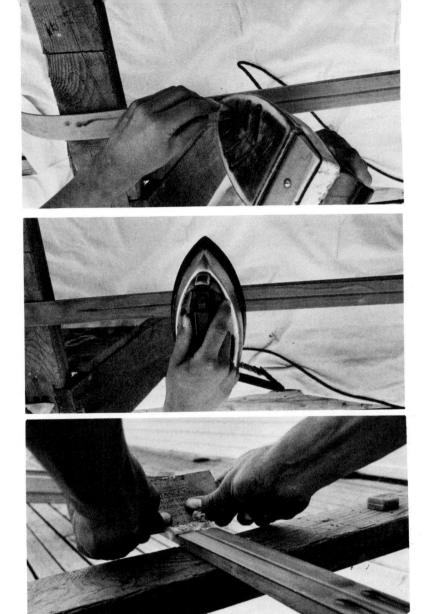

Hot-waxing a fiberglass ski. Top (11), starting to "draw the bead" of speed wax from tip to tail, using a flatiron to melt it. In 12, middle, smoothing the wax with a heat setting right for *Wool*. And at the bottom (13), scraping the wax to a thin film for optimum performance.

Conditioning Fiberglass Skis

each side of the rectangle counts as one, and you can flip it over for four more—which can be sharpened with a file when they get dull. There are lots of scrapers made especially for skis, many of which have rounded sections that are good for scraping the groove. If you don't have a tool for the groove you can round off a corner of the rectangular scraper. Or try a sharpened nail-head, holding it with a pair of pliers; or a sharpened screw-head. We've even shaped and sharpened narrow steel spoons and used them to clean out the groove. Having a groove tool will be helpful in scraping wax off your skis too.

HEATING A SKI

Whenever you use heat on any ski bottom you run the risk of damaging the ski. With the old wood skis many a person used to burn the bottoms when applying pine tar with a blowtorch. Well, there's no need to pine-tar the plastic bottoms, but you still can melt the plastic by using too much heat. If you have had a lot of experience with these new ski bottoms you may have done this already. If you vigorously sand or wire-brush the damaged section there is a good chance you can get rid of the scar tissue and the bottom will be ready for hot-waxing again.

Sometimes it's necessary to use a lot of heat either to apply wax or to clean it off your skis. I've already dealt with the danger of overheating a fiberglass bottom and will just add this for now: Synthetic skis hold heat very well, and you should give them a long time to cool outside before using. Occasionally heat will put some extra camber in wood skis (though the extra bend doesn't last long). If you are satisfied with the camber in your skis and have just finished using a lot of heat on the bottoms, turn the skis over and heat the tops. This should keep things in balance. But be careful not to burn the finish.

In using a blowtorch of any sort great care should be exercised. I've seen so many skis singed, even charred, by skiers who weren't paying attention. The situation with non-wood bottoms can be worse. Some of these don't singe or turn black like wood; instead, they start burning! A hole in a synthetic bottom isn't easy to repair.

After scraping, the bottoms should be sanded smooth. Then if you want the ultimate in smoothness, polish the bottoms with steel wool.

Now they are ready for pine-tarring.

There are at least two reasons for using tar, or some similar substance. First, the pine tar helps seal the bottom. Next, it also helps to hold the x–c wax you apply on top of it (and pine tar isn't the worst stuff in the world to ski on all by itself). I used to tar my wood skis for still another reason: I like the smell of it.

The tars come in instant spray-on, instant wipe-on, and just plain old burn-it-in varieties. Usually the spray-ons don't last as long. Some wipe-ons are very good. But if you want to take the time to burn the base into your skis, this is the thing to do.

To apply the tar follow the directions on the can. You should leave the tar fairly dry after you're done.

DURING THE SEASON

The Bottoms

During the season your Alpine base-wax will wear off the fiberglass skis, and the pine tar will wear off the wood ones. In both cases the bottom will have a whitish look, which you should take care of. Simply scrape the skis clean and apply the base-wax as before.

FIBERGLASS

Or the bottoms of your fiberglass skis may become gouged and these holes should be filled. Clean out the holes by scraping and sanding, or wire-brushing, and then fill the depressions with a Kofix candle—a special soft plastic compound, carried by many ski shops—melted in, or some epoxy glue, or some other plastic specified by the manufacturer. After the filler hardens, sand it off so it is flush with the bottom surface and you're ready to go skiing again.

Waxless ski bottoms may need attention after a few outings even though they're not gouged. Mohair strips can pick up dirt, grease, or even wax left in the track from other skis. Fishscales, ridges and diamonds can get clogged by these same impurities. In both cases, the skis become less effective and should be

Cleaning Skis   41

cleaned. Wipe the ski bottoms with a solvent for wax or grease, to get them back to normal. Now you'll be all set.

WOOD

Wood bottoms will also get rough. They get gouged by sharp objects; splinters are likely to appear; sometimes granular snow is tough on any bottom.

If you have plastic, lignostone or hickory edges, the bottom surface down the middle occasionally wears down, leaving the harder material in the edges protruding and producing what we call "railing." (When this happens you know either that your wax has not been holding well enough to protect the ski; or that you have been skiing in some very coarse snow conditions—which sometimes can't be avoided.) This railing effect is serious. The edges behave like runners and make the ski more difficult to turn or slide around—you'll think they are downhill skis, they go so straight. More important, when the ski does slide sideways there is an increased danger of hooking sharp objects in under the edge and tearing off a section of it. If this happens you're in real trouble, and the best thing to do is get a craftsman to cut out this section of your ski and put in a new little block of wood as a patch.

All these kinds of damage should be corrected by a thorough job of smoothing again. You can be fairly vigorous in scraping wood bottoms: you might get a cup or so of fine shavings. I've seen wood skis scraped so much that the groove is noticeably shallower.

If you're still left with a gouge or hole after this smoothing or scraping, then you should fill the place with plastic wood.

SIDES AND TOPS OF WOOD SKIS

The sides of the ski should be kept clean. Most people don't scrape the finish off the sides; but after it begins to wear off anyway, it's wise to keep the sides waxed. Common paraffin, the stuff used for covering homemade jelly, is fine for this.

The tops get nicked too, after a while. I never refinish the top, but you might want a different appearance. Again, it's a good idea to keep the tops waxed with paraffin. This serves two purposes: It keeps the snow from building up on your skis so you don't have to carry it along with you, and it helps protect the wood from moisture.

Major In–season Repairs for Waxless Skis

REPLACING MOHAIR

If you use mohair skis enough the strips will wear out. To replace the strips yourself, first get the proper sized replacements from your dealer, then pull the worn strips out of the bottoms. It may be necessary to pry under one edge with a screwdriver to get them started. Next, scrape all the glue out of the groove and cut your new strips to the exact length of the old ones. Put a coat of contact cement on the backing of the strips and a coat in the grooves; let the cement set awhile before you put the surfaces together, and then press the strips into the groove.

It is possible to put the strips into the groove too soon and press so hard that most of the cement squeezes out. This won't do. You'll have to pull out the strips and do it right.

An alternative is to let your ski shop make the replacements.

DON'T MESS WITH MACHINED BOTTOMS

If your machined bottoms wear out I would recommend that you turn your skis over to your ski shop for repairs. They will do the job or send them back to the factory.

FIBERGLASS DELAMINATION

Fiberglass skis will delaminate because of poor handling. Like jamming your ski tails down into the snow to prop them up while you take a break from skiing. Or from exposing the slight cracks in the lamination to alternating hot and cold conditions. If a small amount of water gets into a crack, then freezes, it usually expands the crack. Next time more water gets in, etc., and you've got trouble.

And sometimes the glueing process at the factory is not perfect, and the fault can cause a ski to delaminate.

To repair such a ski, bring it in and dry it thoroughly. Then spread open the delaminated area without force, and clean it.

Fill the separation with epoxy, being sure to push the glue in deep, then squeeze the layers together rather gently.

Here is another situation when you can squeeze out all the glue if you try hard enough. But don't. Wrap waxed paper around the repaired area and then clamp it, but not at full pressure: wait an hour before you draw up the clamps to full. After the epoxy dries you should be able to remove the clamps easily from the ski because the waxed paper will have prevented them from sticking to the ski.

For Travel, a Ski Bag

The competitors who fly around the world have always packed their skis and poles in ski bags for ease of transporting. Now, ski bags are becoming popular everywhere for travel by car, bus or train, and I strongly recommend them. They are easy to attach to a car ski rack, hold lots of equipment, and protect the skis from all that junk that flies up off the road during winter travel.

They're easy to make. Get someone to sew up some tough denim or heavy sailcloth; leave one end open for packing, and allow for a fold-over closure or a zipper. Put a carrying handle (or reinforced strap of the material, of convenient length) lengthwise near the middle where the balance is best for you, and you're all set.

Or you can buy a bag.

STORING YOUR SKIS

After the snow season it's best to leave wax on all types of bottoms for summer storage.

One theory holds that a wood ski will better maintain its shape if the stresses resulting from heat and moisture are equal on the tops and bottoms. This is apparently why the skis are lacquered top and bottom at the factory. It wouldn't do to have a wood bottom untreated and exposed to different atmospheric conditions, while the top, because of its finish, remained unaffected. (You probably wouldn't leave one side of a door untreated, unless you wanted it to warp.) Anyway, this is my excuse for not cleaning the klister off my skis in the spring.

Fiberglass skis shouldn't warp on you, but it is important to treat them like new skis before storing. If you leave the bottoms without wax they will oxidize and then next season won't work so well when you go skiing. So, clean them up and iron in a good coat of that Alpine soft wax you used as a conditioner. And this time I wouldn't scrape off any excess. Just leave all of it on for the summer.

I try to store my skis in a cool, dry place, where the temperature won't change radically all the time.

And I do *not* block any of them together. The best reason for not blocking them together and trying to put more camber in them is this, as it was once explained to me: If you can block the skis and put more camber in them, it will be a simple matter to take it out by skiing on them. So blocking won't do any good.

Caring for Ski Bindings

FIRST, MOUNT THEM RIGHT

Bindings should be mounted so that the toe of the boot is approximately over the balance point of the ski. If your shop has not mounted them for you, use the directions that come with the bindings themselves.

With wood skis, mounting bindings is a routine operation; anyone with the right-sized drills and a screwdriver can do the job. But with the fiberglass construction prevalent nowadays a more complicated procedure is usually necessary.

You should know this so you don't come a cropper like the fellow on the Swedish relay team in the 1974 FIS Championships. He had just received a new pair of fiberglass skis—that was the year of the fiberglass breakthrough—and put the bindings on in the usual manner—that is, he drilled holes and screwed the binding on. The trouble was, though, that the inside of the ski was mostly foam. You know, it's lighter, and all that. Well, he led off for the relay, sprinted part of the way out of the start, and popped out of one binding. The meet was in Sweden and all the TV cameras were glued on him as he ran around, looking rather embarrassed, and found a replacement ski. Later on he popped out of the other ski, got a replacement, and was eventually disqualified for taking on *two* new skis.

Since then the companies have been making the skis' innards

out of more substantial material, particularly under the foot where there is so much stress and where you are going to drill holes. The procedure for mounting bindings is simple enough. *But first this warning:* Some glues like epoxy react with the material inside certain fiberglass skis and eat it away, so you should check with your ski shop, or supplier, to make sure you're choosing a glue that will work right for your particular make of ski.

O.K. Drill the holes for the screws, fill them with the correct glue, mount the bindings—and then turn the skis over so they are bottoms up while the glue sets. This way, the glue will pool around the binding screws and harden there—instead of leaking out into an air channel in the inside of the ski, or getting otherwise dispersed.

It's a good idea to lubricate screws with ordinary Vaseline or silicone before putting them into any ski: this makes them easier to take out if a situation ever requires it. However, if the screws are epoxied in, you may have to use heat to loosen them.

IF THE MOUNTINGS LOOSEN

Problems occur when the binding screws loosen. The binding wiggles and the screw holes enlarge. (Have you ever been out in the woods and lost a binding? Good luck!)

If the holes get much too large, stuff them with a wooden matchstick or a wood golf tee and some glue, and re-drill. Or plug the holes completely, and move the binding slightly forward or backward to a new location for fresh screw holes. If the screws come loose just occasionally, plug them with a little steel wool and some matchsticks, then put the screws back in.

Of course by keeping the screws tight all the time you can avoid the trouble of such repairs.

IF THE BOOTS LOOSEN

If the pin holes in the boot sole get too large you can fill them with epoxy glue and re-drill.

Another problem arises when the boot shrinks slightly and does not fit snug in the binding. Then the boot wiggles and, if you have a pin-binding, the holes in the boot are likely to get too large. So check the binding fit carefully. If the boot has shrunk, try hammering in the sides of the binding, or adjusting it if you can. On some bindings this can't be done.

In every case, try to keep a tight fit between the boot and the side of the binding.

Note: You can actually wax your bindings to keep the snow off. There are also some de-icing compounds which keep ice from forming on the bindings and at the same time keep the moving parts loose.

Caring for Boots and Poles

SKI BOOTS

There isn't much difference between caring for x–c boots and caring for shoes, or other kinds of boots. I use either wax polish or a waterproofing material such as silicone on the leather part of the boot.

If the boots get wet, *dry them slowly.* Some leather boots will crack if you bring them in wet and dry them rapidly on the top of a radiator or heat duct. To help in drying you can fill the insides with wadded newspaper or other absorbent material.

Check your boot laces occasionally and replace them if they are worn. No sense fumbling with cold hands out on the trail trying to tie together the ends of busted laces.

SKI POLES

Two situations can really embarrass you.

One is having the handle strap tear or break. You should be able to notice any weak spots in the strap and tape them, or replace the entire strap. I know straps don't tear very often, but if it ever happens to you I think you'll be amazed to find out how much you depend on them.

The other situation is more common, and it's a killer. You guessed it—the basket falls off in the middle of a tour. If you haven't tried skiing in deep snow with a basketless pole you haven't met with one of the ultimates in frustration. So, better check the cotterpin, wire, or whatever holds your basket on. It's safer to replace the parts once a year than suffer out on the trail.

A molded rubber or plastic basket that slips over the tip can be replaced easiest by running hot water over the ring, soaping the pole shaft, and then sliding it on. Don't impale yourself in the process, but you really have to shove when you make the initial move to start the ring slipping down over the shaft. There's no stopping halfway, because you won't make it then. The basket will stick halfway on (and halfway off) and you'll have a tough time moving it in either direction.

You ought to use paraffin wax or de-icer on your pole baskets too. If the basket has wood or leather products in it, waxing also protects them from moisture. More important, wax helps keep the snow off the basket and makes lifting the pole easier.

REPAIRING A BROKEN WOOD SKI

More skiers mean more broken skis, but if we go the route of all-fiberglass unbreakable skis, there won't be this problem. In the meantime, many repairmen are having good luck making a "new" ski from the broken pieces of a wooden ski by using liquid fiberglass. Douse the broken ends of the pieces with fiberglass, stick them together, and then put them in a mold.

The best do-it-yourself mold you can get, especially for a ski-tip job, is to use two sound skis that are the same shape your broken one used to be. Take the bindings off all three skis, wrap the good skis with waxed paper around the area of repair (so they won't get gunk on them); nestle the three skis spoon-fashion, putting one good ski on top and one on the bottom of the broken ski—which is by this time freshly repaired with the fiberglass—and clamp everything together overnight to let the fiberglass harden in place.

The next day you can take the skis apart, sand the repaired one, put the bindings back on, and go skiing.

4: What to Wear

Back in the 1950's when x–c was fairly rare it was easy to identify the serious x–c'er. He almost always wore baggy knickers and carried around with him those long tonkin poles with the big baskets. Some fashion people got hold of the knickers idea (yes, even then) and promoted them for general wear by all skiers.

About the time x–c started its first boom, during the '60's, knickers weren't so special any more, at least with the tourskiers. Whether they wanted to appear special, or whether they wanted to wear any darned thing that suited them, I don't know. But the tourskiers just showed on the scene in any kind of get-up that occurred to them. It's been that way since. There sure are no hard and fast rules for what to wear. Anything goes as long as there is an element of practicality.

Still, I *can* offer a few tips that might help you avoid some uncomfortable situations. After that though, you're on your own.

As I predicted a few years ago that it would do, the clothing market has opened up in North America. It's safe to say that the manufacturers are producing so many different styles and colors that the United States is the world leader in the variety of clothes for x–c. The traditionalists may not cotton to the new designs—which include wild colors and one-piece suits—but they're here to stay. So, as with equipment, if you look around long enough you will probably be able to find anything that fits your needs.

Note: There is more about clothing in Kid Stuff, Chapter 8.

BASICS TO KEEP IN MIND

Before I itemize today's clothing choices there are a few general points that should be made.

Loose and easy. If you are fairly vigorous in your skiing, you should avoid clothing that will bind you. For instance, Alpine stretch pants are out; shirts or tops that might bind you in the shoulders, or behind your shoulder, are out.

Breathing. Clothing made of materials that don't breathe are

14. Right from the classroom to the ski trail, and 15 (right) typical clothes worn by many of the "go fast" crowd.

not too satisfactory. If you perspire very much and you can't get rid of this moisture, sooner or later you'll be cold and clammy.

Weight: Heavy clothing simply isn't necessary if you are going to be moving around enough to generate heat to stay warm. You don't have to dress as if you're in for a long chair-lift ride to the top of some peak.

TWO WARNINGS

First, mountaineers will tell you to avoid sweating if you are going to be out in the cold for long periods of time. With x–c, the problem with sweating comes *after* you ski, when you begin to cool off. If your clothes are wet with perspiration and you stop exercising and it begins to cool off, you may be in trouble. Many cases of hypothermia have been reported as a result of these conditions.

Second, I won't say any more about wind-chill, etc., than this: You should be aware of the fact that wind on a cold day can be very tough on you, even dangerous. You should have a chart available to study for windy, cold weather and you should be careful of prolonged exposure during conditions like this. Having Vaseline to rub on exposed parts like the face is O.K., but it will not protect you from frostbite in all conditions.

OUT ON SNOW

We don't have a very warm house in winter—it's kept at around 65° F./19° C.—and I can wear about the same amount of clothing on a tour that I do sitting around the inside during snowtime. Actually, since I'm so often suited in x–c clothes, it's an easy matter to grab my hat and gloves, step out the back door, and take off. (That brings up another point: lots of x–c clothing is nicely geared for general wear around and about.)

So forget the quilted parka, the mackinaw and those heavy sweaters for skiing, and save them for afterwards in case you'll be standing around or having a long drive home before you can change.

On the other hand, if you're going to suit up in one of those fancy one-piece, form-fitting racing outfits, make sure of being warm by wearing long underwear or keeping on the move, or by doing both. Some of these suits provide little more than a slight windbreak for the person inside them.

On a tour, it's better to take a couple of light shirts, skiing with the extra one tied around your waist until you need it. I would also go with light knickers, and then use long underwear on those cold days when you will really be glad to have it on.

HATS AND EARBANDS

Anyone who exercises quite a bit knows that his head gives off a lot of heat. When I ski, I like a hat or an earband, or both, to soak up some of the sweat, because the more sweat I can keep out of my eyes, the better. At the same time it's important to have material in your headgear that will breathe. You've probably seen skiers come in after a long workout, their hats covered with hoarfrost. This has come from their little old heads, and has just frozen on there.

On real warm days you might not need a hat. If it's mildly cold, you might get away with an earband. If it's very cold, you might want both an earband and a hat. This is a very good combination for bitter weather.

Don't be afraid to overdress in the hat division. There isn't any problem to tucking an extra earband or hat into your pocket, and it might come in very handy for a long downhill run following a warm climb.

16. This stylish grandmother in Reit–im–Winkl, Germany, goes out for a spin sporting cable-stitched sweater, wool gloves and a high-fashion hair-do. 17, lower, shows a motley array of outfits on a Sunday junket—only thing in common: gloves.

What to Wear

SHIRTS AND TOPS

Once again, for x–c a garment's most important qualities are lightness and the ability to let the moisture evaporate. A T–shirt, a cotton turtleneck, a fishnet—each is good. But if you cover these with a nylon shirt you are likely to get pretty uncomfortable. I cover my undershirt with a running top made of a knit material called crepe. It's a stretch fabric and therefore doesn't bind. It also breathes.

In most instances I use just the crepe top (which has a pocket) and a turtleneck. If it's warm out, either the turtleneck or the top will do fine alone. If it's cold and I'm going on an extended tour I might take along an extra windbreaker—a light one—wrapped around my waist.

If I start to get cold I can always move faster and warm up.

GLOVES

Well, my favorite gloves are still those cotton work jobbies affectionately known in Eastern racing circles as "French–Canadien racing gloves." Since writing the first edition, the price of these beauties has risen from 39 cents, but I still find them the best bet on the market. You can go whole hog and get real, ventilated, Finnish racing gloves for around $13.00 at this writing, and there are lots of in-betweens. Some racers have used handball gloves. These also breathe: they're full of holes!

There are lots of mittens addicts. I happen to prefer gloves because they allow a much more sensitive feel for the poling action. However, there's no question that mittens are warmer.

In very cold weather some skiers Vaseline their hands, or rub on some talcum powder; I'm not sure either helps. Another trick is to wear a pair of silk gloves as liners under another pair of gloves or mittens.

If you're desperate for lack of gloves or mittens some day, pull a pair of socks on over your hands. They're better than nothing at all.

KNICKERS, PANTS, OR ONE–PIECE SUITS

Knickers are the traditional x–c pants. They allow the most freedom of movement, and, if you have knicker socks along with them, your legs don't scuff as they pass each other in the stride.

Importance of Layers   **53**

For knickers, I would get light ones. Then, if it's cold, get an old pair of long underwear and cut off the legs just above the knees. This is just perfect for those bitter, windy days.

Warm-up pants are becoming more popular. These were brought in by the racing crowd and were used primarily to warm up in before a race, and to stay warm in after a race. Immediately before a race they were shed in favor of the knickers. Now, since warm-ups feel so good, lots of skiers use them instead of knickers. If they are fairly snug around the lower leg they don't allow any scuffing. And, if you're going to stand around a lot, as coaches do, they're better than straight knickers, being warmer. Wear 'em myself.

These are traditional items, remember. But—while I wouldn't go so far as to recommend bell bottoms—lots of other combinations are possible. If it's warm, shorts are just great. Or you can try the "Putney springtime uniform"—long underwear with shorts on top. It's very fast on the downhills because there is so little wind resistance. (I haven't seen many x–c'ers in leotards, but they would be fastest of all!)

One-piece suits are becoming very popular now, even with tourskiers. They come in two basic styles: full length, which have a strap under the foot (and with which you wear short socks) and regular below-the-knee length, which require the traditional knicker socks.

The suits are made of a stretch material and do not bind if they fit properly. Since there is no air space around your midsection, as with knickers and a regular top shirt, these suits are warmer than knickers and tops made of comparable material.

I wouldn't be surprised if one-piece suits soon dominated the market.

SOCKS

If you have knickers you're sort of bound to use knicker socks. If you don't, you'll get mighty cold. Wool socks are the best since they are warm and shed the snow very well. There are other lighter, tighter-fitting socks and you pay the price for this lightness. You don't stay as warm, but if that's not a problem, O.K.

These days, most of the racers wear their second pair of socks, if they wear them at all, inside their knicker socks. The skiers on my team used to chide me when I wore mine outside. It dated me, they said. That's the way it was. When I want to look older and wiser, I still wear them outside.

If you're wearing long pants and don't need knicker socks, you should try the so-called thermal socks. I've had good luck with them.

I've seen some skiers wrap a plastic freezer bag over their socks before the boot goes on. If they're going out in real wet weather, or know they're going to get wet feet, they claim this helps.

AVOIDING COLD, WET FEET

It's easy to get wet feet, and this is the complaint I hear most about. Skiers' feet can even sweat enough to get socks and boots wet, to say nothing of the snow and other elements working on your feet from the outside. There are a few precautions you can take to help avoid this problem.

1. *Gaiters,* which are becoming very popular. These fit over the top of your boot at the ankle. The biggest job they do, I think, is to keep the snow from going down inside your boot; snow seeping in here is the surest way to get wet feet. So, if you're going to be skiing in deep snow a lot, you should invest in a pair of gaiters. They come in many sizes, from very narrow on up to knee length.

2. *Boot-gloves have come on the market too.* Made of a rubberized material, they keep your boots dry. You can slip them on and wear them satisfactorily in most pin-bindings. Of course these won't work with the new Adidas type of boot-binding combination.

3. *Put a pair of old tight-fitting socks on right over your boots.* This is an inexpensive way to keep your feet warm.

4. *Polish your boots regularly; or use waterproofing compounds.* Either will help to repel moisture from the outside—and it goes without saying that dry boots mean warm feet.

5. *Allow your boots to cool off when you step outside your door to go skiing.* Stand still a minute or two in the cold air before rushing right into the snow with warm boots; otherwise the snow will melt on your boots and you'll be on your way toward wet feet.

AFTER SKIING

The best thing to do after a tour is to dry off and keep warm. If you have a shower and a change of clothing available, that's fine. If you don't and you're stuck somewhere, there are a couple of things you can do.

I suppose the most welcome item after a workout is a dry T-shirt. If you can bring one of these along with you, jump right into it. You might even want to rub yourself off with snow first. It's very refreshing.

If you don't have any extra clothing to change into, try this. Switch the order of your shirts. Sometimes the outside shirt is the drier, and you can put that on right next to your skin. Put the wet one on the outside—and maybe it will dry soon too.

GOGGLES AND PACKS

Until recently, the use of goggles in x–c was always considered a No–No. The problem used to be that the goggles steamed up so much that you couldn't see out of them.

But now they've improved the ventilation system enough on some models to make fogging no longer a problem. At any rate a few skiers are using them.

If the sun is very bright and you're going to be out a long time, you could wear goggles with dark lenses to protect your eyes. Sun-glasses are better, however, and I would recommend them, especially in the spring when the sun gets higher and brighter. You also might invest in one of those elastic bands that go around the back of the head to keep the glasses from slipping off when you're really moving.

A good item to have is a fannypack. Also called a kidney pack, it is a shaped pouch that straps around your waist and is worn out of the way below the small of your back. You can put extra wax, corks, snacks, socks, etc., in one of these and carry it along with ease on your outings. They come in several sizes.

Note: There are some more tips in Chapter 12—Going Out for All Day.

What to Wear

5: Some Notable X–C People

One of the greatnesses of cross-country skiing is the wide diversity among the people who love it, for they reflect all aspects of the sport and come from all walks of life. During the quarter-century or so that I've been associated with the international x–c scene on both sides of the Atlantic there have been plenty of heroes and heroines, and here I pay tribute to some North Americans who have inspired thousands of others with their enthusiasm.

18. A century on x–c skis: Herman Smith–Johannsen between Eva Ohlsson of Sweden, left, and Shirley Firth of Canada.

First on anyone's roster of notable x–c'ers is Herman "Jackrabbit" Smith–Johannsen of Piedmont, Québec, 101 years old as, in the photograph here, he poses—typically flanked by two beautiful girls—in March 1977 for "friend Caldwell from Vermont." On his right is Eva Ohlsson of the Swedish National Team. On his left is Shirley Firth of the Canadian Team; she and her twin sister, Sharon, dominate women's x–c in North America.

19. Rudi Mattesich has been spurring interest in recreational cross-country since the 1960's as head of the Ski Touring Council, based in Troy, Vermont.

Born 15 June 1875 near Oslo, Norway, he was on skis by the age of two, and when he came to Canada in 1902 to sell heavy railroad machinery he cruised much of the route to be taken by what is now the Canadian National Railway, often traveling on x–c skis accompanied by Cree trappers on snowshoes. His name among Cree Indians is *Okawacum Wapooes*—"Chief Jackrabbit." The world's most famous veteran cross-country skier has behind his home a two-mile loop that he still covered almost every day of the 1976–77 snow season, in addition to skiing to the post office for each day's mail.

Two of his numerous formal honors came in 1972, when he was made a Member of the Order of Canada, and he received a medal from King Olav of Norway.

All x–c'ers start somewhere and many of them get additional encouragement through such outfits as the Ski Touring Council, headed by Rudi Mattesich of Troy, Vermont 05868. In later chapters you will see how very little children can get their first enthusiasm for x–c in casual outings with their families. These youngsters quite often develop into being skilled competitors on their school teams, perhaps eventually finding berths on Junior national teams before graduating to Senior status.

Some Notable X–C People

20. Personifying *The Sound of Music* in the Green Mountains: Baroness Maria von Trapp.

Another source of pleasure—and experience—is any of the now almost countless x–c touring centers (more on these later too) which are springing up each season. One of the best known is the operation run by the Trapp Family Lodge in Stowe, Vermont, and developed by Maria von Trapp.

And not to be overlooked are the many open, or citizens' races, throughout North America. A prime mover in these events is Eric

21. Dr. Eric Barradale at an early Washington's Birthday race. After starting a field that included first-graders and 70-year-olds—with possibly several moonlighting Olympians—he'd go over to check the finishers.

To Inspire Tourskiers

59

22. John Bower, who became Nordic Director of the U.S. Ski Team in 1975, shown here before he won the men's jumping/x–c event at the 1968 Holmenkollen.

Barradale of Guilford (again Vermont: but this state has been a hotbed of x–c activities in the United States for almost two decades). He instigated the Washington's Birthday Ski Touring Race in 1963—a friendly competition open to skiers of all ages and abilities, where the oldest and youngest finisher got as much applause as the over-all winner.

23. Bill Koch, wearing his favorite number, en route to his silver medal at Seefeld, Austria, on 5 February 1976.

Finally I present two racers whose achievements have never been equaled—at this writing—by other North Americans in international competition. One is John Bower, who won the King's Cup for Norway's prestigious Holmenkollen Combined in 1968. The other is Bill Koch, who electrified the x–c world by winning the 30–kilometer silver medal in the 1976 Olympics.

Holmenkollen and Olympics   *61*

6: Technique

The most fun in x–c skiing is moving around the terrain any way you like, and personal enjoyment should be your most important consideration. However, I feel there are many recreational skiers who like to work on their technique and this chapter is written for them. I am describing the classic form here because I think it is a more efficient way for them to ski than using the latest racing technique, which requires a degree of strength and stamina not possessed by the usual tourer.

If you are a family skier and want to work at it, I'm sure you can learn to go fast over certain sections of the track and get that thrill of speed which comes easily with the proper technique. If you're a racer you should read the more specialized approach in my other book on training and technique.*

But if you want to do your own thing and ski your own way, just skip this chapter and no one will be the loser. I'm serious about this.

A NEW APPROACH—AND WHY

In this edition I'm going to put forward a new method, or you could call it a new chronology, for learning to ski x-c. I wrote about this method once in *Skiing* Magazine, but other than that I have given it very little publicity. Nevertheless it has become my favorite way of teaching beginning skiers.

This new system starts out by emphasizing certain arm movements.

Hey, wait a minute! you say—the *legs* are the most important parts of the body in skiing!

I agree. So I'll say it too. The legs are the most important limbs in skiing x–c, and provide by far the most strength, power and stability. I merely emphasize use of the arms in this method because I think it's a good way to learn. For the following reasons:

1. *In beginning to learn a skill sport, most North Americans*

* Caldwell on Cross-Country: Training and Technique for the Serious Skier. *The Stephen Greene Press, 1975.*

are far more adept with their arms than they are with their legs.

You recall the old trick of testing arm *vs* leg co-ordination by throwing a ball to someone: If he catches it with his hands, he's from North America; if he traps it with his feet he's from Europe. This difference occurs because of North Americans' ingrained preference for such games as baseball, basketball and our brand of football, as compared with the Europeans' being brought up on soccer, where touching the ball with your hands is a No–No unless you're the goalie.

Thus I find that North Americans generally have good control of their hand and arm movements—which makes it quite easy to teach them basic x–c skiing movements by starting with emphasis on the arms.

2. *This system is probably unique.* Which makes it fresh. And fun.

You can read about the traditional methods that stress leg movements in my earlier books, or in other people's books for that matter; there are also lots of professional ski-touring groups in the U.S.A. and the Dominion which have good methods for teaching. All the ones I know of put prime emphasis on the legs, and start you off with a walking or shuffling motion.

So there's no dearth of information on x–c technique, and I don't really want to argue the merits of various teaching systems. I have already written about the traditional methods. I thought I'd simply offer another approach this time around.

3. *And finally, the important thing is to be able to teach something—not the method that's used to teach it.*

I guess my bag is education, and if there's one thing I've decided after a quarter-century in the field is that you can teach a thing in any number of ways. My new approach, therefore, is offered not as an end-all, but rather as a way that might work well with a lot of skiers who are new to x–c, or who are teaching their friends or families.

On the Flat

WHAT YOU'LL ARRIVE AT: THE DIAGONAL STRIDE

A well-executed diagonal stride is the hallmark of a practiced x–c'er. You've seen pictures of a good skier in full flight: right arm reaching out ahead to set the pole, matched by the forward-driving left leg; left arm and right leg extending backward, almost parallel. If you drew lines from arm to arm and from leg to leg you'd see why we call this x–c signature "the diagonal."

Although the stride is a natural elongation of walking, if you're like me and try too consciously to correlate these movements, you

---

TIPS FOR THOSE FIRST TIMES OUT

Millions of people in North America are enjoying x–c: skiers touring in deep powder in the high country, or backpacking on skis through the forest, or traipsing across a pasture, or even racing like the wind along a well-packed trail. However, don't be misled into thinking you are going to reach these heights first time out. Remember, all those skiers in the pictures started out just like you: they all had a first day. And perhaps it wasn't so easy for them, either. But they probably used discretion, took some simple precautions, and came back eager for more. Here are a few hints that may help you:

Start out skiing in tracks. This will make everything much easier for you. Slogging through deep snow is heavy work for anyone and it makes learning to ski quite difficult. After you gain experience you will enjoy the deep stuff more.

Go out with a friend, an instructor, or someone who knows the ropes. Follow his lead.

When you begin to tire, stop. You may discover muscles in your lower legs, for instance, that you never thought you had. They can tire rather quickly just from trying to maintain your balance. After a few times out, though, you'll be amazed and pleased at how much you progress.

Be sure your equipment fits and is in good shape. Nothing is worse than trying to ski with skis that don't slide or are too long and awkward, or with boots that twist around in your bindings, or with boots that are too big and don't give you good control over your skis.

Dress warmly in the pants division, using long underwear if it's cold. Wear several light shirts, including a wind-breaker, and shed them according to the weather and your level of exercise.

---

may get all mixed up. But if you master the steps—meaning the stages—described below, you'll be well on your way. Thereafter it's only a matter of lots of practice. And your work will be repaid, for a good diagonal combines power (provided by the thrust of legs and poling action) with moments of relaxation as the limbs swing forward once more.

Technically speaking, nearly all phases of hill-climbing—as well as flat skiing—use the diagonal: that is, alternate legs and arms move in a co-ordinated fashion.

Note: This technique sometimes is referred to as the "single stride." I use the term myself but I can't explain its derivation: what would a double stride, or even a triple stride, be like? Probably rather difficult maneuvers . . .

There are four steps in the following sequence leading up to the diagonal, or single-stride, technique. The diagonal will remain the classic method of traveling on x–c skis for a long time to come, despite a slight trend away from it in the racing camp. This is the stride that you will use in judging your own proficiency— or another skier's. This is the one you will most enjoy practicing, or skiing with, too.

STEP ONE: THE DOUBLE–POLE

Are you ready to go? I will assume that your equipment is ready and your skis work—that is, they are waxed correctly or are waxless skis that work in the given conditions. I will also assume that you are skiing in tracks, packed out especially for x–c skiing.

The first exercise takes place on the flat or on a very gradual downhill. It's called double-poling, and you simply reach forward slightly and place both poles in the snow at enough of an angle so that, when you push down on them, the force will propel you forward along the tracks. Keep your elbows close to your body.

You may find you don't have enough strength to do this. If so, you'll have to train your arms gradually and build them up. Meanwhile, you can try this exercise on a slightly steeper downgrade where you can coast without pushing on the poles. Begin coasting, then give a push with the poles to get the feel of it. After a few times you'll have the ability to go back to the flatter— i.e., less steep—downhill.

Double-poling, no steps. In the left one (24) note the positions of the body and the pole-plant to get maximum force for 25 in the middle; then (26) poised to do it again.

TRY IT UPHILL

After your arms get stronger you can try double-poling on the flats—and then, believe it or not, *up* some gradual hills.

If you are a teaching purist you're going to get after me right now and ask how in the world this poor skier can get back up the hill if I haven't taught him how to walk or climb.

That's a good question and I'll answer it this way: This sequence is aimed primarily at teaching the single stride, or diagonal. I would hope that the teacher or the reader (pupil in this case) would get the whole sequence in mind before going out, and so perhaps would be able to apply the next steps to get back up the gradual hill.

I'll admit this will not work with some beginners. With them, there are two choices left. You let the beginner improvise. You might be surprised at what he will be able to do to get back up that little old hill.

Or you tell him to take off his skis and walk back to the beginning point.

STEP TWO: SINGLE–POLING

Here comes a really good builder of co-ordination and strength. In it you propel yourself along the track using just one arm at a

Technique

27–32. Single-pole exercise. It takes strong arms to propel yourself along the flat without using your legs (sitting back a bit is natural).

time, alternately, while you keep your skis steady, like a sled's runners.

Place each pole at an angle so the force will propel you forward as you push down and back on it. In this poling motion you should begin to think about pushing each arm far enough to the rear so that your hand passes by your thigh.

Again, it will be easier to start on a gentle downgrade. If you progress so you can do this on the flats, then on gradual uphills, you will have developed excellent strength and co-ordination,

Toward the Diagonal

33–35. Here is the one-step double-pole. This is like the exercise in Photos 24–26, but with an added leg movement. Practice so you can move ahead on either leg.

Technique

both of which will come in handy doing the diagonal stride. However, it's not necessary to be able to do this exercise uphill before proceeding to the next step.

STEP THREE: ONE–STEP DOUBLE–POLE

In this exercise you reach forward with both arms simultaneously, as in the double-pole, and at the same time, slide one ski forward. Then push with the arms.

Practice so that you can slide either leg forward, and pole, using both arms forcefully. A good drill is to alternate your legs. Start with the left ski sliding ahead, pole, then coast a bit; slide the right leg ahead, double-pole, and coast. Continue.

At this point you may begin using your legs for some power. As you double-pole, give a little push, or bounce (here called a

---

GETTING UP FROM A FALL

Some people have difficulty getting up from a fall or are afraid to fall. In either case, skiing is made less enjoyable—which is too bad. Because almost all falls in x–c are O.K. They don't hurt. In fact, you can gain a certain confidence in falling without fear if you do fall occasionally. I'm not telling you to rush out and take a winder; but if you are a worrier, try to change your attitude. When you do fall remind yourself that it wasn't too bad after all.

Getting up from a fall is easy. First, if necessary, you should untwist yourself, then get your skis together and pointed in the same direction. To do this you may have to lie on your back and swing your skis over you up in the air, keeping them parallel. If you're on a slope be sure your skis end up below you and across the hill.

Next, hunch up a bit, or assume a fetal position, then get on your knees and push yourself up with your hands, which are braced against the snow or against your skis.

It is often a mistake to try to hoist yourself using your poles. This becomes too much like a difficult pull-up, or the poles sink and you slither back down onto the snow. You might even want to take off your poles before you get up.

A beginning diagonal might look like this (36–38)—slightly restricted in movement but combining the basics learned in the first three stages.

kick), off the leg you did not slide forward. If your skis aren't holding, or if you push too hard off this more stationary leg, your ski will slip back. If this happens, don't push back so hard with the rear leg. Instead, try pushing (kicking) *downward* more.

REVIEW OF 1 THROUGH 3

A review is a good idea at this time. Make sure you can do the three preceding exercises fairly well. Pay attention to your arm-swing, so it is relaxed as it goes forward and there is enough extension beyond your hip as the arms push to the rear. I ask my skiers to continue pushing back with the arms, whether they are using them one or two at a time, so that I can see some daylight between their arms and hips.

STEP FOUR: THE DIAGONAL ITSELF

To do the diagonal simply reach forward with your right arm and at the same time slide your left leg ahead; pole with your right arm and give a little push off your right leg. Then reach forward with your left arm, slide the right ski ahead and push with your left leg.

39–44. A polished diagonal will enable the skier to cruise along, extended yet relaxed, as in this sequence above and below. Maintaining a forward body position requires leg strength and balance. And practice— but it's all worth the effort.

It's like walking. You alternate: right arm and left leg ahead, left arm and right leg behind.

If you've followed the sequence leading up to the diagonal, you haven't concentrated much on using your legs. But you ought to begin now. As you pole, give a slight push down and back with the more stationary leg—which has completed its glide and is

45–50. Getting up from a fall: Above and opposite, the skier is head first downhill—the hardest position to get up from. So he lifts his skis in the air, swivels so he can set his skis below himself at right angles to the slope, and uses arms and poles to get up and get going.

ready to extend behind you—just as I suggested you do in the one-step double-pole.

When everything goes well you will glide a bit on the forward ski, then reach forward with the other arm and slide its opposite leg ahead simultaneously, pole, and push off the stationary leg, and soon you've got it. After a while you will gain some rhythm and will be able to glide along in near effortless fashion.

HOW TO CORRECT COMMON DIAGONAL FAULTS

The more accomplished you get with the diagonal, the more likely you are to acquire a few individual stylistic flourishes that will keep you from feeling too mechanical. Don't worry about them; they'll distinguish you from an automaton. For instance, I seem to cross one arm in front of my body, but not the other. And we had one boy on the U.S. Team who ran with his head cocked to one side.

The basic rule to follow in using the diagonal stride is this: *Try to make all your movements directly ahead.* Use economy of motion by making only those movements which contribute to carrying you straight along the track.

Technique

The following are a few common faults that should be guarded against in the diagonal because they can keep you from getting the most out of your effort. They don't spoil your enjoyment when you're out cruising around, but they can add up to disappointment in a competition.

Not enough drive forward. To improve, you may have to develop more strength and balance. Skiing is the best way to do this. You can try skiing occasionally without poles. This helps the balance.

Not enough extension. To correct this, concentrate on driving the front arm out straight—e.g., reaching forward with your pole without bending your arm. Although most skiers don't use a straight arm out front, the straight arm sometimes is helpful in getting better extension.

Upper-body bob. If someone watches you ski from the side he can tell how much motion of the upper body you have. As the better skiers glide along the flats, their heads stay at just about the same height from the track all the time. Others bounce up and down in their strides and eventually wear themselves out— or get sore backs.

To eliminate this bob, try relaxing your back, even to consciously rounding your shoulders slightly at the end of your glide.

Diagonal Remedies

51. Skiing without poles—a good drill to help improve balance. Try this in narrow tracks, and so what if you tip over in the snow?

Side-bending. This could be a balance problem, and it's easy to spot by having someone sight on you from directly ahead or behind. Sometimes if the tracks are too far apart, or if you are skiing too much on your edges instead of on the flat of your ski, you will bend from side to side with each stride.

Sometimes it happens because you swing your arms too wide, instead of straight ahead.

Skiing without poles will often remedy this situation, especially if you use tracks that are very close together, so close that your bindings hit each other occasionally. Then, if you side-bend too much, you will tip over into the snow. Soon you'll learn to stop bending.

Hanging the rear leg "out to dry." If you ski with a fast tempo, there is hardly time to leave that leg out there, to the rear, so if you're one of those fellows who lift their rear leg too high, try skiing with a faster tempo.

It also will help if you concentrate on keeping the rear foot as close to the snow as possible. This in turn can be helped by pointing the rear hand downward toward the snow as you finish your poling motion. (Racers are so conscious of this that they seem at full extension to be holding that rear pole with only thumb and forefinger.)

DOUBLE–POLING AS AN END IN ITSELF

One of the most important changes that has taken place in the racing scene has been in the area of technique. The new skis and the new waxes are much faster than before, the tracks and courses are faster, and all these factors lead to an increased use of the pure double-pole and the one-step double-pole. You won't see the diagonal stride used so much by racers as it used to be, particularly on the flats.

Even though you will use the single stride with diagonal poling most of the time you'll want to practice your double-poling for certain conditions. On gradual downhill sections of terrain, or on fast icy snow, on flat parts of the trail, or before making step turns (discussed under "Downhill"), the double-pole is a fairly easy, natural maneuver.

The success you have with double-poling will depend on your balance and your strength. Some strong skiers with good balance almost throw themselves out over the lead ski, both arms reaching forward, and then give a tremendous thrust with the poling motion by using their arms, shoulders and body weight. Others will not have the balance to venture so far forward.

There are lots of variations of double-poling as used by individual good skiers, but it would take too much space to describe them here. Work out whichever modification suits your style and strength.

One good hint I can give, though, is that you try to get your body weight into the poling motion. This means not pushing too hard until your arms are bent—and then, when they are bent, sort of sinking down on the poles with your weight as you push.

Uphill Skiing

Skiing uphill under your own steam is one of the hallmarks of x–c. Here is a place where the many unique features of x–c combine to give you a great deal of satisfaction. The equipment is light and allows that freedom of movement which is necessary for

52–57. Above and opposite: Straight uphill requires skis with good purchase. By tipping this sequence down to the right (so the skier seems on the flat), you can see the similarity between straight uphill skiing and the beginning diagonal of Photos 36–38. But in skiing uphill the body is crouched over—even accordionated—more than in flat skiing.

almost all uphill skiing. The practiced x–c'er, is, I dare say, a trifle stronger than his Alpine counterpart, and therefore able to exert a bit more strength to get up hills with ease. And, finally, the properly waxed skis, or the waxless skis, provide that extra in grip, or purchase, which enables you to go straight up some of the fairly steep slopes.

There are almost as many different ways to ski uphill as there are degrees of steepness. The good skier uses different techniques with varying amounts of effort, depending on the slope. I'll hit on half a dozen of the methods.

USING THE DIAGONAL STRIDE

If the uphill slope is relatively flat and your skis grip well, and if there's a good track and you're feeling strong, you can glide up the hill using the plain, old, on-the-flat, diagonal technique. To get some glide going uphill takes quite a bit of strength, and sometimes it's helpful to assume a slightly crouched body position.

Technique

Be careful not to sit back in your crouch here, though: your weight should be forward for maximum purchase. Failing to keep the body weight forward is one of the most common faults of skiers going uphill.

Bounding—More, or Less

If the slope is steeper—but not so steep that you have to sidestep or herringbone (see both below)—there are several techniques that may serve.

The most energetic is the bounding stride used by racers when they're in a hurry. They practically leap from one ski forward onto the other. The amount of extension depends on the slope, the skier's strength and his wax; but in general he extends less than in his diagonal stride on the flat.

The Shuffle

The shuffle, long regarded by racers and coaches as used only by skiers with poor balance, is coming back on the racing scene. The reason for this is that the shuffle is probably the best way to get up most hills during a race. Yes, the racers are catching on to this most rudimentary of skiing movements, perhaps the one you used when you began skiing.

I can give you a few hints about this technique but you'll have to make the fine adjustments yourself after some experimenting. First, be sure the slope of the hill is not too steep and that your skis have good purchase. Then, standing fairly direct over your skis, shuffle along, trying to keep the skis in maximum contact with the snow. Concentrate on driving, or shoving, the legs ahead —one at a time, of course. Naturally, you will have to set your wax or your waxless ski bottoms with the shuffle of each forward ski, and to do this may require a slight movement, or compression of the body, and some co-ordinated poling action. But the trick is to avoid as many bouncing-up-and-down motions as possible. If your skis are holding well, jumping up and down on them as in ski-bounding just wastes energy. The hot racers on the international circuit discovered this a while back and that is why they are using the shuffle so much now.

If you are waxing up for a long tour, a good guide to use is the shuffle. If your wax enables you to shuffle, you'll probably be O.K. for the trip.

Dog–trot

The third method, which I'll call the dog-trot, is good for fairly steep slopes. In this one you lean forward a bit more, assume a fairly low body position, and take rather short steps.

The key to this dog-trot is a "soft" ski out front. By that, I mean you cushion the step by bending the ankle and the knee. The knee should be right over, or even ahead of, the foot. It's as if you're sneaking up the hill, or you're trotting along on a bunch of fresh eggs, trying not to break them. It's important to keep your body weight forward. If you get back on your heels and have to rock forward onto the ball of your foot in each step, you'll soon get tired.

The poles should be used with a minimum effort. If it is necessary to pole hard with each step, or to hold yourself from slipping with each step, then (a) you should be using another technique, or (b) you need more purchase, or (c) your weight is back too far, or (d) you're not doing it right in the first place. The poles should be used almost as an afterthought.

Another way of thinking about it is to imagine yourself running, or dog-trotting, up an inclined cement ramp, with sneakers

Technique

58–60. Here's one I'm good at—the sidestep. Beginners should find this a sure method for getting up a hill.

on. If you wanted to jog up the ramp in the most relaxed manner, how would you do it? Chances are you'd dog-trot.

SIDESTEP

The sidestep is a sure, easy way to climb. Stand with your skis across the slope, or at right angles to the fall-line. (The fall-line is the route a ball would take if it could roll freely and unimpeded down the hill, which means it's the most direct way up a slope.)

Then lift the uphill ski and move it up the hill a foot or so, digging in the uphill edge as you put it down. Now lift the other ski, place it beside the upper one—and you should be a little closer to the top of the hill. Continue.

TRAVERSE

The traverse is probably the tourskier's most common method of getting up hills. It is really nothing more than a diagonal, or single, stride with a bit of the sidestep effect thrown in.

Skiing up a slope with linked traverses is similar to taking a zigzag road to the top of a mountain. To start traversing, get crossways to the fall-line and, as you move your uphill ski for-

61–63. More uphill. Here the positions of the skis and poles—plus the telltale tracks—illustrate the herringbone.

ward in the single stride, slide it slightly up the hill; then slide the other ski alongside and ahead. Thus you proceed forward across the slope and upward at the same time. The poling motion is identical with the diagonal stride.

To change direction, link one traverse with another by getting into a herringbone position (described below) and sort of crabbing your way around. Then start upward across the slope again.

HERRINGBONE

The herringbone is a very quick, but tiring, method of getting up hills that are too steep for your diagonal stride.

Your legs and arms alternate, exactly as in the diagonal, but there are some important differences. First, there's no glide (unless you're a superman!); second, your skis are splayed out in a "V"—which, repeated, produces a herringbone pattern, hence the name; and third, in order to hold from slipping, you must really dig in with the inside edge of each ski.

If you're strong and in a hurry, this is it. (It is a very important racing technique, since many of the hills on a competition course are so steep. The U.S. Team even has dry-land drills for this one.)

Technique

As a last resort, you can always take off your skis and walk. Don't laugh. I've been in races when I was so tired and my wax was so bad that I know my times would have been faster if I'd taken off my skis and walked. I would have been disqualified of course, so I grunted it.

But you don't have to keep 'em on. You're out for fun, and x–c is your own thing. Right?

Downhill Skiing

There are really two basic situations you'll come up against with your downhill skiing. Either you may be on a trail, following some sort of packed track that doesn't give you much room for choice, or you may be out on your own on an untracked hillside, where you can use lots of different ways to get down.

I'll cover trail skiing first.

THE TRAIL: STRAIGHT DOWN

The fastest, easiest way is straight down. Assume a relaxed, upright position, with weight evenly distributed on both skis; keep flat-footed—and go. If you want some extra speed you can crouch over and rest your forearms on the tops of your knees. This tuck cuts down wind resistance and also is restful.

Be careful of the tuck when the slope is bumpy, however, because it's a hard position to hold if you're bouncing around. On rough going, it's better to straighten up. But don't be stiff and rigid: relax.

It's possible to go very fast on x–c skis. In races, on some steep downgrades, x–c skiers get going at least 60 kilometers per hour (about 35 mph), but you can be sure they've got their eye on a nice outrun at the bottom. I'm not recommending such speed for you. I do say, though, that you should always be able to see your outrun when you're going straight down a hill—otherwise you may be headed for trouble and not know it.

Because it's no good to take a chance on bumping into something like a tree or another skier, you'll need a few other methods of controlling your speed and direction of travel. Like the following.

64. A relaxed position for a straight downhill run: crouched, with hands crossed and forearms resting on knees.

THE TRAIL: STEP TURN

The step, or skate, turn is the most efficient method of changing direction in any kind of skiing on any kind of skis. Just raise one ski slightly off the snow, point it in the direction you want to go, set it down, lift the other and bring it alongside the first.

Naturally, the faster you are going the faster you have to move those skis. In fact, some x–c runners often practice high-speed turns by jumping off the snow with both skis and landing with them pointed in a different direction. This can be difficult, but it's a very neat way to change direction.

THE TRAIL: SNOWPLOW TURN

Snowplowing is possible under most conditions and it has the advantage of being more controlled than straight downhill skiing: you control not only your speed, but also your direction.

In doing the straight-down snowplow, be sure to keep the tips of your skis fairly close together while pushing your ski tails apart in order to get that edging or braking action. To turn from this position, weight or push harder on one ski, and this force will drive you around in the desired direction.

There are a couple of more informal ways to slow down which I'll cover in a minute. Meanwhile let's hit the open slopes.

Technique

65–69. For going downhill, do it your way. Stand up straight, flex at the knees or waist, crouch or tuck—and wear what you want to!

Going Downhill

70–72. A step turn (which was preceded by a double-pole). In the last shot above you'll notice the arms swinging into position to pole again.

This snowplow—coming down where I herringboned up—is only fair. At top · and center (73 and 74) I'm O.K., but in the bottom picture (75) my right ski has slipped back to a straight-down position and therefore is not an effective brake.

Technique

OPEN SLOPE: TRAVERSING DOWN

Naturally, when you have a whole hillside to yourself you can use all the turns mentioned so far. And there's a special beauty too. With so much more freedom of movement here, you can lay your own course between and around obstacles, and there are no compulsory corners.

Absolutely the most pleasurable way I know of for going downhill in open terrain is by using the traverse. I like to head down at an angle just steep enough to keep me going. This way, I get the maximum distance out of the slope in return for whatever climb I made up to the start of the downhill piece. I recommend it as effortless, ideal for easy step-turning, and giving you the bonus of time to enjoy the scenery as you go. And it's so quiet that you can often sneak up on animals.

OPEN SLOPE: TELEMARK TURN

The Telemark turn is very graceful and most appropriate for powder skiing. It was developed long before the present-day resort slopes were packed out with such maddening efficiency. So the Telemark nearly went out of style when the Alpine boots

76–78. Powder snow and the year's first Telemark turn. (To see how it finished up, see the next sequence!)

Turning on Open Downhills

79–84. Continuation of the author's first Telemark turn of the 1976–77 season, started in Photos 76–78. Notice the problem approaching in the first shot: the eggbeater grand finale (opposite) was inevitable.

and bindings became so restrictive as to prohibit its use (you need that heel-lifting freedom you get with x–c gear). Then, only a few x–c skiers carried on the tradition for years. But now, with many more x–c'ers skiing everywhere, there is a practical need for it, especially in powder, and I'm happy to say that this classic turn is coming back.

To do it, slide one ski ahead of the other as you go downhill. Slide it so that the binding of the forward ski is about alongside the tip of the following ski. Then stem the forward ski—to the left if it's your right ski that is ahead—weight it or edge it slightly, use your arms for balance, and you should go around. Bring your skis together to complete the turn.

Don't worry if you fall. It happens all the time. But after you master this turn and can link a number of them together going down a slope, you will be something to behold.

The turn can be done at very low speeds. At higher speeds it's a bit more difficult. And, as I said, it's great for powder skiing.

BUT ANYTHING THAT WORKS IS O.K., REALLY

Since writing the first book I have heard of a few, but very few, broken-bone accidents in x–c skiing—one in particular being a

Technique

collision between two skiers. But bone breaks are still very rare. Usually the equipment breaks before a leg gets enough stress to do so. This is a marvelous safety feature in x–c, because new equipment is a lot cheaper than doctors' fees.

Your gear will survive informal maneuvers, however, like the following. Even pride won't suffer—if you keep loose.

THE BUSH–GRAB

A friend of mine has developed a technique that's probably unique among ardent x–c'ers for negotiating some of the slopes around Vermont. He is an acrophobiac of the first order and, short of going downhill blindfolded, has perfected the bush-grab. Carefully he gauges his speed so that, when he gets near enough to the first bush on his course, he can grab it and come to a stop. He then heads off for the next bush or tree. After a trip through tree country he comes in covered with twigs and birchbark, pleased as Punch with himself and the world.

It's good to report that, as the years go by, he's cut down on the number of these braking stops.

THE SIT–DOWN

If you get in trouble downhill, don't be too proud to sit down and scoot on your fanny to a stop. Start by easing your weight

Do Your Own Downhill Thing

85. Kind of a show-offy way to change direction: the *Quersprung*, in open terrain.

down so you can drag your hands in the snow on each side—like twin stabilizers—to keep from tipping over sideways. Then gradually let your body sink into the snow, slightly back and to one side or the other.

AND THE FALL

I still get comments about my controlled, though impromptu, fall as shown in an earlier book of mine.

If you find yourself in the middle of an unpremeditated fall, and the landing area is soft, try to save your skis. The preferred fall is one in which the skis pass backwards under your body, don't dig into the snow, and don't break. Think of it as a Bicentennial spread-eagle instead of a belly-whopper if you want to.

Technique

7: X-C for the Handicapped

As cross-country skiing grows, you can expect to hear more and more about skiing for the handicapped. My first contact with their participation in snow sports was watching amputees zooming down some Alpine slopes with their outriggers: you may have seen some of them too, at least on TV. I'll confess I didn't think much about how the handicapped could ski x–c until I came up with some very minor injuries and was faced with the prospect of not being able to ski for a while myself. Then I was pleasantly surprised to find what I could do with my leg in a cast.

Since then I have run into more and more handicapped skiers and am happy to report that x–c is well suited for them. In fact, the handicapped often develop so strong a desire to ski and exercise that their input could be the envy of many racers in training.

While I am by no means an expert on these matters I hope that my observations and the information I include here will provide just another spur in the development of skiing, x–c especially, for the handicapped. I'll apologize right now if my use of certain terms like "paraparetic," "partially-sighted," etc., is not consistent with everyone else's definitions. I have found some discrepancies here and I can only tackle them to the best of my ability.

AMPUTEES

Most people agree that below-the-knee amputees can perform quite well on x–c skis. There is little question that Alpine skiing with outriggers on each arm—ski poles with very short skis on the bottoms instead of baskets and points—plus the aid of gravity, makes this an easier sport than x–c, but if you're an amputee and want to do x–c, you'll be able to.

Above-the-knee amputees unquestionably will have more difficulties, and should start out on very easy terrain. After that, several factors will enter into determining what can be accomplished—the natural ability and strength of the skier, snow conditions, the track itself, the terrain, and so on.

Again, in general, Alpine skiing will be easier for most am-

86. Junior-high boys from the Austine School for the Deaf (Brattleboro, Vermont) starting on x–c.

putees since the over-all level of conditioning is not so high as that required for x–c. Some amputee Alpinists consider themselves as skiing better than 70 percent of the physically normal skiing population—and with good reason.

THE BLIND

There are some good programs for the blind, a few of which I will describe below. Suffice it to say that almost all blind people need a guide to accompany them: it's a one-on-one situation. I say "almost all blind people" because there are some skiers who know certain courses well enough to be able to tour 10–15 kilometers on their own. And you may have already guessed another vital need for blind skiers: good, deep tracks which serve to guide the skis.

It's pretty hard to imagine yourself in the position of a handicapped person unless you are one. But here is a situation you can simulate, slightly. Just put on a blindfold next time you're out and see what it's like to ski this way. If you do this and think it's difficult, then try to imagine how it would be if you had balance problems in addition, as many blind people do.

87 and 88, two *Ski for Light* meets. Above, blind skier Marcia Springston and her guide, Olaf Johnsen, after taking part in the 1977 program in Woodstock, Vermont. Mary Patrice Newman of Oklahoma City and her sighted guide, Monica Andersen (bib 139), in the 1976 x–c program in Lakeville, Minnesota.

The Blind

Guides or instructors for the blind are often blindfolded as part of their training. In this way they can understand the problems better, and thus can communicate better with their students.

The Partially–sighted

The partially-sighted have approximately the same needs as the blind in order to ski x–c. However, they are judged to have some advantages over the blind and, in most of the races they run in, they are put in a separate division.

It's generally agreed that skiing x–c is easier for the blind or partially-sighted than skiing Alpine.

PARAPLEGICS

The Boston Marathon has featured a special Wheelchair Division in this, the most famous marathon run in the United States. In 1977 the wheelchair entries started 15 minutes ahead of the field and the winner arrived at the finish having been passed by *only 30* runners.

I never imagined that paraplegics could do anything comparable on x–c skis but there are specially made fiberglass sleds which serve the same purpose as a wheelchair. The skiers use shortened poles and propel themselves around with tremendous double-poling. In some competitions the paraplegics have more than held their own against racers with other handicaps, such as blindness.

Paraparetics

There is not much information or experience I can report about paraparetics—people who have partial paralysis of the legs—but in talking with some who ski Alpine, they sound confident about wanting to do x–c. I'm going to look into this and may have something to report in a year or so.

In the meantime, I would appreciate any information you can send me.

THE DEAF

Skiing x–c may seem like a straightforward situation if you're deaf, but it's not all clear sailing. The way one paraparetic ex-

If you have skied much downhill in deep, icy tracks, you know that it's possible to attain very high speeds and have difficulty even getting out of the tracks to snowplow. You usually end up hanging on for your life—or bailing out of the tracks and taking your chances in the crust at the side. The first time I saw the drags pictured here was on a trip to Germany in 1977 (where these photos were taken), and I must admit there were some times when I wished I had them.

89. The ski instructor put these rigs on his skis (above) at binding level. There is a spring-loaded hinge which keeps the claws, or drags, in place during normal skiing. But when he wants to slow up—as on a fast downhill—he simply pulls the cords (Photo 90, below), which are attached to the claws. The harder he pulls, the more drag he gets and the slower he goes.

I don't think many racer types will take to these, but then there are always the rest of us.

These contraptions could be used to fine advantage by anyone with a lower-body handicap, or by everybody who's leery of fast downhill stretches.

Brakes for Your Skis   93

plained it to me exemplifies the fine attitude displayed by so many of the handicapped: "Boy, am I glad I'm not deaf, because so many of those people have equilibrium problems!"

There are many x–c races scheduled for the deaf; in fact, many deaf skiers enter regularly sanctioned races in the United States. The distinguishing mark of a deaf skier is a special armband, and the signal for passing—if you happen to be fast enough—is tapping his ski pole with yours instead of shouting "*Track!*"

READY TO HELP

Most handicapped people snort at anyone who even begins to feel sorry for them; this is especially true of those who get deeply involved in sports and recreation. Some studies show that involvement in these areas helps to produce a very high level of success in professional occupations like medicine, law, etc.

But then there are the handicapped who either do not know of the possibilities open to them, or who are reluctant to try something in sports, for instance. These are the people who need encouragement and this is one reason I give a list of organizations to contact right here.

Note: To date there are not many full-fledged programs for instructing handicapped in x–c. Many experts feel that the handicapped themselves will eventually become the best teachers, but there have not been good training programs for them. In the meantime there is a need for instruction and if you are interested you should get in touch with one of the organizations listed below and offer your services.

National Handicapped Sports and Recreation Association, attention of Fred Nichols, Penn Mutual Building, 4105 East Florida Avenue, Denver, Colorado 80222.

Among other things, this organization sponsors the National Handicapped Skiers Championships. The first x–c race in this yearly series was held in 1978 at Winter Park, Colorado.

New England Handicapped Sportsmen's Association, 29 Woodcliff Road, Lexington, Massachusetts 02173.

Here is a very active group that can provide a lot of information about numerous programs in the East.

National Blind Organization for Leisure Development (BOLD), 533 East Main Street, Aspen, Colorado 81611.

BOLD was founded by Jean Eymere, a former member of the French Olympic Alpine Team. Jean is a diabetic who lost his sight and then decided to promote Alpine skiing for the blind. Since the establishment of BOLD, which still emphasizes Alpine skiing, Jean has taken up x–c and trains seriously for the Ski for Light races. At his home in Aspen, he goes out without a guide and skis as much as 10–20 km with ease, a feat not many sighted people can match.

Ski for Light, Inc., c/o Sons of Norway, 1455 West Lake Street, Minneapolis, Minnesota 55408.

One of the leading events in the United States is a race for the blind run under the Ski for Light program, which is sponsored by the Sons of Norway. Each blind skier has a guide or instructor who works with him in preparation for the race. They practice on the course—which has two parallel tracks so they can ski side by side—and work out audible signals for the race.

Mike Gallagher, many times Champion of the United States, was chief of race for the 1977 running, held at Woodstock, Vermont. In commenting on the race Mike said he was amazed at the speeds attained by the blind skiers. He cited one or two cases where the guides got in over their heads and couldn't keep up with the handicapped racers.

At this race there were 91 entries, divided into three classes: blind, partially-sighted, and physically (motor) handicapped. There were only two in the physically handicapped class but one was a paraplegic who won his division handily and defeated over half the field as well. His equipment was a fiberglass sled, shortened poles—and a pair of super-strong arms.

The interest in this whole program has grown, with six regional races planned for 1978. You can get more information from the address above.

Finally (for now) there is the *U.S. Deaf Skiers Association,* Simon Carmel, adviser, 10500 Rockville Pike, #405, Rockville, Maryland 20852.

For leads to counterparts of these groups in the Dominion, write to the *Canadian Ski Association,* 333 River Road, Place Vanier, Tower "A," Vanier City, Ontario K1L 8B9, Canada.

8: Kid Stuff

Lots of queries come to me from parents who want to know how to get their kids into x–c skiing. No two family situations are exactly alike, of course, so it's hard to prescribe any standard approach, but I'll summarize some of my observations and experiences.

ADVANTAGES

The advantages of getting kids into x–c should be pretty obvious:
1. *X–C skiing is a natural activity for children.* It's the next thing to walking, and chances are that kids don't have hang-ups about balance, or fear of falling, etc.
2. *X–C is very learnable compared to Alpine skiing.* After a few minutes, or a few times out, most kids will be on their way to a workable competence.
3. *X–C can be immediate.* If you live near snow you can go out with practically no fuss and bother—which means that kids often get a chance to capitalize on their current whims or desires.
4. *X–C is more available than Alpine skiing.* If you can find some snow almost anywhere, x–c is go. No lift tickets to buy; no wait at lift-lines.
5. *X–C equipment, being more flexible and comfortable than Alpine gear, makes x–c more attractive to kids.* And an x–c outfit is much less expensive.

PHILOSOPHY AND GUIDELINES

The basic approach should be to make it fun for kids. Every time you plan something for a youngster, or a group of youngsters, ask yourself how you can make it fun. If your primary concern is getting kids out of the house for a while, or if x–c for them is some part of a baby-sitting arrangement, you probably are on the wrong track.

My mother-in-law once asked me when I thought kids ought to start skiing and I told her, "Just before they learn to walk; that way they won't develop any bad habits in form."

91. Some youngsters get their first exposure to x–c being towed in a *pulka.*

Well, I was putting her on a little. But we did get our children going as soon as we could, and in all cases they were clomping on skis around the living room floor well before age two.

You might not be in the right circumstances to do anything like this so I'll suggest that you start your kids on x–c skiing as soon as you can find equipment for them.

FOR LITTLE ONES

With very young kids—from age two up to eight or ten—it's important to make x–c skiing a family thing. You know how kids are, often in need of a parent or an older brother or sister to help them out. Most of them are accustomed to having some family member around at all times and it's only natural to have it that way when they ski.

Make x–c skiing an adventure for kids. There are all sorts of games you can play, depending on their age. Hide-and-seek may sound a bit corny to an adult since it's pretty clear that anyone can follow ski tracks and find someone who is hiding. But that's just the point. The little kids really love something like this—for many it's a discovery, and they learn in the process.

A Family Thing 97

So almost any game you play on foot will adapt itself to x–c. Just go slowly with it, assuring some degree of success for the kids who are playing the game, and chances are they'll enjoy it.

FOR SCHOOL AGE

As kids get older you can take them on short jaunts. Anytime you can inject a practical element or a goal into a situation, you have a good thing. We used to ski over to visit a neighbor who had invited us for a little party. And our kids actually skied to school —I know this is one of those things you read about and never quite believe, but it was a case of their skiing or our having to drive them. They liked school, so you can imagine I tried to make sure their skis were well waxed every day for that trip.

This introduces a couple of other concepts. In skiing to school our kids acquired a certain degree of independence, they over-came the vagaries of all sorts of weather, and they gained confidence in plain x–c skiing and in their ability to master physical activities. They also learned that x–c skiing is practical.

In setting up x–c skiing for kids you will discover increasing opportunities to pose a challenge for them that they will delight in meeting. It can take the form of skiing to school, going on a tour through hitherto unknown terrain to a friend's house, an inn, another ski area, a lean-to, a picnic site, a good view, a cabin, and so on.

Through it all, keep this x–c thing low key. So the kids didn't want to ski to school one day? No big deal—pack 'em in the car and drive them.

Or they don't want to go touring. That's O.K. too. Next time just try to make their x–c experience something they will enjoy more and will want to do again. You know how kids are: if something is fun, they'll do it.

EQUIPMENT FOR KIDS

First, an important point. Go to your dealer and insist that he try to get some kids' equipment if he doesn't already have it. Small-sized gear is made in Europe and it is available, but many dealers in North America don't think there is a market for it. Well, a few years ago they didn't think there was a market for

92. Parental involvement: go along, encourage—and keep a light touch.

x–c stuff in general. So if you can prod your dealers it might help to get more equipment on the market for youngsters.

THEIR SKIS

In getting equipment for children make sure the skis are not too long. The old standard of having the skis reach your wrist out-

93. A warm drink makes a pleasant break during an outing on x–c skis.

stretched above your head isn't applicable to kids. Their skis should be about as long as they are tall, no more. They can paddle around on them more easily.

Waxless skis are probably the best bet for a child. Since they work most of the time without waxing, everyone—parent and child—will be happy.

THEIR BOOTS

The boots should be flexible and something that youngsters can wear for other occasions, for two reasons. First, if kids already have their x–c boots on during those winter days and an urge to ski hits them, they are all set to go. Sometimes overcoming a small obstacle like finding boots and putting them on can discourage any kid.

The second reason is a practical one: maybe the kids can get

94. Here's another version of today's one-piece suit. And notice the goggles he'll need on the downhills . . .

some wear from the boots before they outgrow them. We tried to keep our kids in their boots until the things wore out, even using them on mountain climbs and summer hiking trips.

I would recommend the standard x–c boots and bindings for kids, if you can get them. There are some ski and binding combinations that fit galoshes or hiking boots but these are O.K. only for very young children if you can't get the traditional equipment.

THEIR POLES

The poles ought to be a bit shorter than the armpit length that is standard for older skiers. Kids never seem to have much trouble bending over and they can make a pole work even if it comes somewhere between their waist and armpit.

HOW TO BEGIN

Kids will need a lot of attention getting started in x–c. However, it's not necessarily instruction they'll need. In fact, I've advised a lot of parents not to try and teach their kids, or not to let their kids see them ski too much for fear the kids might pick up bad habits. Give the kids assurance; watch them, encourage them, cheer them on. This will do more than anything else in the beginning.

But above all, don't *hover*. Don't give them the idea you're riding herd on them—or that they've got to please you, for heaven's sake! Heavy-handed parental gung-ho can ruin any sport for a kid. So when I say "watch them," I mean to be available always to encourage the child who wants you to.

Start on the flats and gradual downhills. Walk along with them, prop them up, or straddle them with your legs and guide them. Uphills will be a problem, but if you are patient with them on the flats and downs for a while, even pulling them back up the hills, soon you will be rewarded and they will do the uphills by themselves. Naturally, having waxless skis—or waxed skis that work—is important for the uphills.

Probably the best single piece of instruction you *can* give them is how to get up from a fall. As soon as kids are confident that they can get up themselves they'll be a long way toward skiing

---

EXCHANGE PROGRAM

In my corner of Vermont a good source for kids' equipment is the annual exchange of winter-sports gear put on as a money-raising affair, and chances are that there's a similar event in most places in the snow belt. This is how the yearly venture, held the week before Thanksgiving, is co-sponsored by the Brattleboro (Vermont) Recreation Department and the Brattleboro Outing Club:

People who have skis and clothing to sell bring the articles in to a central place on Friday, having set their own price on each item. The sale is Saturday, and the following Monday the people come by to collect their money—less a percentage that goes to the sponsoring groups—or any items that didn't find a buyer. The sponsors split the percentage, using the money for special programs.

Good bargains, fun, and a boost for worthwhile community projects.

Kid Stuff

on their own. But until then they will get stuck in all sorts of awkward situations and will need help. One year one of our kids had boots that were too big and every time she fell down she came right out of them (the ultimate in safety features!). Since she didn't yet know how to put on her own boots this did cause a problem. You see, we did start them young.

If the skis are short, as I advised, kids will be able to roll right over on their backs, flipping their skis overhead and bringing them together. If they flop the skis downhill, or below them, and then get on to their knees, they will be able to push themselves back into a standing position. If they want to use their poles to hoist themselves up, that's fine, but it's not necessary. It may be easier without poles.

If kids have a chance to observe good skiers, just to see how it's done, they'll catch on. They are marvelous mimics. So I wouldn't advise any formal class instruction for them until they are fairly well advanced in technique, or just yearning for instruction. The best thing they can do is play games, take small trips, have fun fooling around and playing follow-the-leader, and being in an unstructured situation.

There is an increasing number of good x–c films out now and showing these to kids is another way to improve their skill and enjoyment of the sport.

THE TORGER TOKLE–BILL KOCH LEAGUE

For several years the Eastern Ski Division of the U.S. Ski Association has sponsored a league for kids' Nordic skiing—that is, in jumping and x–c. The original league was named after Torger Tokle, a famous ski-jumper who was killed during the Second World War serving in the U.S. 10th Mountain Division in Italy. After Bill Koch's Olympic silver medal in 1976 the name of the league was changed to recognize his feat as well.

Many teams in the league are well organized and coached. They begin training during the fall, and have fund-raising drives to buy equipment, and in general go the club route.

Parental involvement can be very constructive here. After all, someone has to help drive the kids to meets, pick up their bibs, wax the skis, get the kids organized, and so on. In fact, even during some of the training sessions we find parents right up there in the workouts, learning such things as hill-bounding, roller-skiing

95. This young racer displays good form—and it probably came from watching others.

and specificity exercises. During the summers some parents lead trips in the mountains. All this is good.

I hope the league stays this way and that it remains low key and that the race schedules don't get too imposing. I worry about the "Little League Baseball syndrome"—parents screaming at their kids, at the umps, at the coaches, and all that. The minute ski parents get competitive, or worry too much about their kids' times, or insist on certain training sessions, or get upset about missing the wax, there's going to be a bummer.

The most important thing to remember is that x–c is a marvelous lifetime sport. Let's not do anything to discourage anyone from enjoying it as a recreation.

9: Waxing

The waxing of x–c skis used to be one of the great mysteries of skiing. Few newcomers to the sport could understand how any substance applied to a ski bottom would enable one to go *up* a hill. And of the people who did accept this notion, few knew what waxes to use or how to apply them. It was no wonder that many skiers were turned away from cross-country skiing.

Many of the competitive groups did little to help the situation either, keeping secret, with a skill to be envied by the CIA, their special wax combinations used for races. Some teams hired in wax experts for the bigger, more important races, virtually locking these wizards away in isolation for many hours before the meet. No movie-going or bar-hopping the night before, not by a long shot.

This whole situation changed very gradually, and a few years ago, just before the advent of fiberglass and waxless skis, things seemed to have leveled off. Most x–c'ers were taking to waxing and doing a reasonably good job. There were lots of treatises on the subject and even more waxes available. Waxing had almost become an accepted part of the sport.

But now we're off and flying again—in many different directions. There are large numbers of waxless skis; there are wooden skis with wood bottoms or plastic bottoms; there are fiberglass skis with different bottoms. And ski companies have done little to co-operate in recommending standard waxing procedures for similar types of skis.

The total amount of knowledge necessary to be able to wax every type of x–c ski in any condition has increased several times in just a few years. Fortunately, however, the physical process of applying wax is getting easier and easier. So if you are content with taking the simplest approach to waxing and if you stick with just one kind of ski, then it becomes easier than ever before. On the other hand, if you are waxing for a competitive event you'll virtually need a computer in order to handle all the different possibilities.

I'll hit the basics for you and then will mention some of the refinements used by top competitive skiers. And instead of combining comments on waxable and waxless skis I'll deal with the waxless models first. They are certainly the easiest—and it *is* a good idea to wax them occasionally.

TIME OUT FOR A GLOSSARY

If you're reading about x–c waxing for the first time, it might be a bit confusing to meet terms like "klister," "binder," and such, so let me stop right now to give a few definitions. They'll mean more to you as you read on, but I think they will be easier to refer to if I set them down here. Nor will it hurt anybody if the information is repeated later in a different way.

Alpine waxes. See *Glider* or *Speed waxes.*

Base waxes. Usually these are soft Alpine waxes used on *fiberglass* skis to help seal and protect the bottom. Or they can be pine-tar compounds used to help preserve wood skis.

Binder waxes. Any wax used to help purchase waxes and speed waxes adhere or last longer; therefore, all binder waxes go on before purchase and speed waxes, and then are covered by them. One of the best-known types of x–c binder is called *Grundvax.*

Cork. The cork used to be a chunk of actual cork, for smoothing wax that's been daubed on the ski. However, nowadays a cork is a cork or something synthetic. But at least its use remains the same.

Corn snow. Granular snow that has started to melt and therefore is wet. It can be just a trifle moist, or quite wet—depending on the temperature.

Cushion wax. A soft wax applied under the foot (the mid-section of the ski) that snow crystals can indent, thereby giving purchase. A cushion is usually covered by another harder, and therefore usually faster, purchase wax. Not used on waxless skis. See also *Kicker zone* and *Purchase waxes.*

Frozen granular snow. This is cold, dry, harsh snow that has melted at least once and refrozen. (Westerners refer to it as "Eastern Powder Snow.")

Glider waxes. Speed waxes, usually made by x–c wax companies.

Hard waxes. Purchase waxes used primarily for powder snow. They come in small "tins" or containers. Before application they give the appearance of being "harder" than klisters.

Hot-waxing. The method of ironing speed wax or base wax onto the skis.

Iron. Actually, any piece of metal used, when warmed, to melt and smooth wax. Household irons and special waxing irons are the most commonly seen.

Kicker zone. That part of the ski under the foot where purchase wax is applied. Often it is determined by the paper-sliding test for flexibility described in Chapter 2, Equipment. Also called the *kicker strip.*

Klister snow. The stuff you use klister wax on—almost always snow that has melted and refrozen. There are two categories under this one: frozen granular snow, and corn snow.

Klister waxes. Purchase waxes used primarily for granular snow conditions. These waxes come in the tubes, are very sticky, and, if you get things messed up just right, can remind you of an underdone taffy-pull.

Paraffin. Especially in the U.S.A. and Canada, the soft wax used to seal homemade jellies, etc.; comes in slabs from the supermarket.

Powder snow. Until the winter of '77, something that was thought to occur in North America only in the western part of the continent. Light, fluffy, soft, and cold.

Purchase waxes. These are waxes, usually applied to the midsection of the ski only, that provide purchase, grip or climb. Sometimes referred to as *kicker waxes.* They are not used on waxless skis.

Speed waxes. These are waxes used to make the skis slide easier. Often called *Alpine* or *Glider waxes,* they should be used on waxless skis and are optional for waxable skis.

Spray waxes. Usually speed waxes, but occasionally purchase waxes, which can be sprayed onto the ski.

Techniques of Waxing

WAXING WAXLESS SKIS

I've talked with executives of waxless ski companies and most of them will admit that waxing their skis occasionally is a good idea. But they don't want to be quoted on it—yet.

It should be obvious that you don't need purchase wax on these skis. The mohair, or the design machined on the bottom, is there to provide you with the necessary grip.

Still, you should use speed wax regularly on sections that do not contain mohair or the machined design. Speed wax will make the skis slide forward easier and it will also help to protect the bottom surface from wear and oxidation.

Furthermore, if you are careful you can put on speed spray, speed wax, or paraffin (the most basic kind of Alpine wax) on the whole ski, as long as you apply it in the direction of tip to tail. You can see why this is important. If you rubbed wax on from tail to tip with a step-type ski like the fishscale, it would clog the gripping edges and make them less effective.

Applying Speed Wax to Waxless Skis

Before you start any waxing, be sure your skis are clean and dry. No wax will work well if it is put on over little flecks of dirt and water. In fact, most waxes won't even stick to a wet surface.

The method most often used for applying speed wax in cake form is to rub it on. Corking the wax to smooth it is O.K., but don't cork the area that contains the design. Another reminder: Do it from tip to tail.

If you have an iron handy and want to drip the cake wax on, then iron and scrape (as described in Chapter 3), this is fine. You'll be best off doing this in a warm room; and of course you'll avoid dripping wax on the design section.

You can use spray waxes almost anywhere. They are the easiest to apply. They are also the most expensive. And you had better not let many of the ozone group see you discharging that stuff into the atmosphere.

One of the most popular waxes for mohair strips is WD–40. This compound helps to prevent icing, and experienced skiers are never without some of the stuff. Silicones are good for this too.

HOW OFTEN

Here are the ways you can tell when your skis need more speed wax:

1. Those whitish spots or streaks begin to appear on the ski

bottoms, or the whole bottom takes on a paler hue.

2. You have cold-snow wax on and the weather turns warm, etc.

3. You are using the same model as someone else and your skis are a lot slower.

4. Run your fingernail along the bottom. If you don't come up with any wax, it's time to apply more.

CHOOSING SPEED WAX

If you want to keep it simple, get hold of a cake of wax for cold snow and one for wet snow. If the cakes are too big to carry in your pocket while skiing, break them into smaller pieces. It doesn't take much to wax a pair of skis.

Back in my early jumping days we always used paraffin for speed. The market wasn't flooded with all the present-day varieties of Alpine waxes and spray waxes, so most of us used Lebanon White for every snow condition. When it was warm we put on a rough coat of White; when it was cold, a thin, smooth coat. Lebanon White was readily available: you see, it's nothing more than the paraffin used on preserves.

Don't laugh. I try to get my skiers to have wax boxes of their own and in a fit of generosity I often help to get their collection started by donating some Lebanon White. I still use it, just the way I did in the '40's.

You can use it too. It's cheaper than anything on the market.

If you have a good background in Alpine waxing then you may want to get hold of several brands of speed wax and proceed from there. I don't recommend this for the average tourskier, though. The difference between a universal cold-snow wax and one more specialized according to a narrower temperature range is not that significant for touring. Keep it simple. Furthermore, waxless skis are generally slower than waxable ones, so if you want to be that much faster you should consider switching skis.

WAXING WAXABLE SKIS

Applying Speed Wax to Waxable Skis

You can use the same techniques for applying speed wax to waxable skis that I described above for the waxless skis. However,

Techniques of Waxing   *109*

you should leave the kicker zone free of speed wax so that you can apply purchase wax here. In fact, in very cold, powder-snow conditions you'll probably be better off applying hard wax (purchase wax) to the whole ski and forgetting about the speed wax. Hard waxes are plenty fast enough, sometimes faster than any speed wax the average racing coach can concoct, and these waxes have the added advantage of providing you with more purchase.

Some Variables in Purchase Performance

Several years ago when x–c was new to so many people, the main consideration was getting some climb, or purchase, and it was assumed that any wax you selected would be applied to the whole ski. Today, however, waxing for purchase, kick, climb, or whatever you want to call it, is not just putting something on the ski bottoms and going out. There are several variables, and an understanding of these will help make you a better waxer.

Generally, *the thicker you apply the wax the more climb you'll get.*

LENGTH OF KICKER ZONE

The longer your kicker strip is, the more purchase you will have. The extreme is to wax the whole ski with a purchase wax, and, so long as the wax is not slow, this is fine. Lots of skiers still do this, and it offers the utmost simplicity in wax selection.

The other extreme comes from some racers who try to use as short a kicker as possible, sometimes on the order of 10 centimeters (4 inches). This way they can use speed wax on the rest of the ski and be faster on the downhills.

The use of purchase wax, or fast x–c wax, on the whole ski *vs* hot-waxing the tips and tails with Alpine wax, is one of the debates going on now in the racing world. In general, not much, if anything, is gained by using Alpine wax on tips and tails in very cold, powder conditions. Many racers dispense with the Alpine wax and use some brand of Special Green x–c wax or other special x–c running or glider waxes. One claim for using this x–c wax is that it makes the skis more stable in the track.

SKI FLEX

Some skis are stiffer than others and this flex plays a vital part in the performance of any wax job. Just imagine a ski so stiff that when you press down on the mid-section, where you have waxed for purchase, it does not come in contact with the snow! You won't get much climb with *this* ski.

It follows that your ski should be the right flex for you (see how to test for flexibility in Chapter 2). If it is too stiff, you will need a longer kicker strip and a thicker coat. If it is too limber, you will not need so much wax—but it will wear off more easily.

For klister conditions racers use what is called a double-camber ski, and it works this way. A flex pattern is built into these skis so that, when a racer rides both skis evenly, the mid-sections do not press down firmly into the track. Thus the runner is riding primarily on the tip and tail sections, where the Alpine speed wax has been applied. When the racer kicks such a ski vigorously down into the snow, the pressure is strong enough to set the wax, or give grip.

These skis possess such an extreme stiffness that tourskiers are advised to stay away from them. You must be very strong and in good condition to make them work. Leave them to the racers.

SKIING TECHNIQUE

Some skiers kick down very hard, while others have what I describe as a more gentle, long-drawn-out kick. The stronger skier with the harder kick generally can get away with less-thick purchase wax and a shorter strip of it. The gentler type of skier may need a longer strip of wax, but might be able to use something a bit harder or faster—assuming both skiers weigh the same and have identical skis, etc.

WAX AND SNOW CONDITIONS

It goes without saying that your choice of purchase wax and the existing snow conditions have a lot to do with your skis' performance. Nuf sed.

METHODS FOR APPLYING PURCHASE WAX

There are several different ways to put purchase wax on your skis. The most important consideration is getting a smooth, finished coat on a clean, dry surface. You'll soon develop a favorite method of application and should stick with it as long as it continues to work for you.

Use of Heat with Purchase Waxes

Using heat to melt the wax, or soften it to make smoothing easier, was considered bad form by some purists several years ago. I always went ahead with heat anyway because it was a lot easier. And I never had any trouble with the wax's performance.

Now the use of heat is almost universally accepted. This doesn't mean you must use heat to wax, or that you can use it without certain precautions. If you use an iron for hard wax be sure it is just hot enough, and no more, to do the job, which is to smooth the wax out. A temperature of about 140° F./60° C.— right around the *Wool* setting—is usually recommended. A too-hot iron will cause extreme melting: The wax may run into the groove (thereby causing your ski to "swim" as it fails to track straight, or causing a build-up of ice in the groove); or the wax may run over onto the edges of the ski. Also, a hot iron can damage the ski bottom. These same cautions hold true for torching any wax.

With klisters it has always been a favorite trick of mine to melt them in a pot over moderate heat and paint them on (see below). This is O.K., but take care that the klisters don't begin to smoke. Occasionally I've left the mixture on the stove too long and it has caught fire. Not good.

Applying Hard Wax

I'll list some methods for applying hard wax and give brief descriptions of each.

Rub and cork. This is the standard method. Rub the wax on your kicking area, or longer if you want, and smooth it out with a cork. If you do this in a warm room you will usually have good luck in smoothing the wax. The smoother the wax the better it will perform for you, uphill and downhill.

Rub and iron. Rub the wax on and smooth it with an ordinary flatiron, as above, being careful not to force wax into the groove or onto the edges of the skis.

Rub and rag. Rub on the wax as before, then heat it with a torch and, using a rag scrunched up into a little ball, smooth the wax on one side of the ski groove, then the other. The size of the rag ball might be no bigger than is necessary to cover a dime or quarter. If it's small, it will soak up some wax, you'll have better control of it, and smoothing will be easier.

If you rub too hard you will force the wax into the groove or over onto the edge. It takes a delicate touch and most skiers enjoy this kind of art work.

Melt and cork. You can "melt" hard wax onto the ski bottom and then cork it. Melting can take two forms: either you hold the wax against a hot iron and drip it on, or you warm the wax by holding it against an iron or near a torch, and actually rub it on. If you drip it on, it will take longer to cork in.

Melt and rag. As above. The most common method is to heat the wax and rub it on, then rag it in, using heat from a torch.

Some skiers use various combinations of these methods. You could rub wax on, iron it, then rag. And so on.

Applying Klister

Klisters are the most maligned waxes in x–c. So many skiers have had problems applying klister that they have gotten discouraged and, in turn, have discouraged others about waxing in general. Poor misunderstood klisters!

With decent waxing facilities and a little practice you will be amazed both at how easy it is to apply klisters and how well they work. Klisters almost always climb better than hard waxes, by comparison. Rarely do you slip if you have the proper klister for a given condition, whereas with the proper hard wax for a given situation, you are always bound to slip now and then, or on a steep uphill.

Here are the standard methods for applying klisters. As always, you should wax in a warm room with a warm wax, and your skis should be dry.

Apply with heat and paint. One neat method is to put the klister on your ski, drawing two beads for the length of your kicker strip. Then heat it gently with a torch and paint it smooth. Care must be exercised anytime you apply pressure—as with a brush—to soft wax in order to keep it from running into the groove or over the edges.

Apply and rub. Apply the klister as above and then, using the

Techniques of Waxing 113

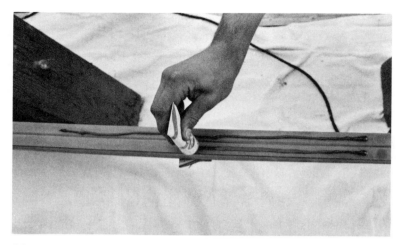

96. Drawing a bead of klister on the kicker zone, then (97, below) smoothing it with a plastic scraper.

meaty part of your palm right below the thumb, smooth it out. If you wax in a warm room with warm wax, no other heat should be necessary. You can probably get the best control over wax thickness, etc., using this procedure. But many people don't like to get their hands sticky and therefore shun this method.

Apply and smooth with a scraper. Apply the klister as above and then use a scraper to smooth it. Some companies provide an excellent plastic scraper with every box of klister; but you can also use a metal scraper. You'll have the best luck if you work on one side of the groove, then the other. Don't pull the scraper with too much pressure or you'll spill the wax off the running surface.

Cookpot method. Punch a few holes in your klister tubes and throw them in a pot to heat and the klister will ooze out. Grab a paintbrush and apply the wax.

The cookpot method is marvelous for applying mixes. If you want a 3–to–1 mixture of Red and Silver simply put it into the pot. This method is about the only way to klister large numbers of skis efficiently. As I advised above, heat the klister not quite to a smoking point, then take it off the heat and paint it on the ski.

How Long and How Thick

After you have selected a kicker wax—i.e., purchase wax for the kicker zone—the main question that remains is, How long and how thick should it be?

I can give you an estimate, but you should work final details out for yourself by experimenting. Keeping a little waxing diary, or some such, will prove invaluable. Most tourskiers apply kicker wax from a point behind the heel, and going forward, up the ski toward the tip, for about 60–80 cm.

You should experiment with kicker strips by shortening them, moving them forward or back with respect to the center of the ski, etc.

For comparison, racers these days begin waxing at the heel, or even slightly forward of that point, and use short strips, averaging from 30 to 50 cm.

There really is no firm rule for determining the thickness of a wax coat, but I always begin with an "average" coat of hard wax, which is one I can easily see after it is smoothed yet not so thick that I can scoop it off in gobs with a fingernail. Then, if I need more climb I can add wax, making a thicker coat.

I put klister on so it's a little thicker than a good coat of paint. Usually it's better to have it thicker than thinner (see below).

Techniques of Waxing

How Often

Hard waxes will last for long distances in the right conditions. I've skied over 100 km on some wax jobs.

The rule with hard waxes is easy: If the wax still works, leave it on. If it's worn off a bit, patch it up. If a newer, softer wax is called for, you can apply it directly over the old wax. If a newer, harder wax is called for, you should clean your skis and rewax.

Klisters are a bit different. They pick up dirt, bits of hemlock cones, pine needles, leaves, etc., quite easily and after most one-day trips you will have to clean them off and rewax. However, if the klister looks relatively clean and it still works, use it.

How to Choose a Wax

In the earlier editions of this book I drew up wax charts—but don't look for them now: I've dispensed with them, for several reasons. For one, the usual time-lag between writing something and seeing it printed always seems to give the wax companies time enough to come up with another new wax, or even two. So my charts were slightly outdated before they were published. I notice now that many wax companies have given up the practice of printing those handy little wax charts many skiers used for easy reference.

Next, the charts and all such may have led skiers to make too much out of wax selection by a brand name. One frequently hears comments to the effect that, "Oh, if you had only used Brand X Blue instead of Brand Y Blue . . ." and so on. Most often, if someone has a problem with waxing it is because he did not apply the wax properly.

Finally, most skiers now possess a higher degree of sophistication about waxing and I don't think they need a chart to tell them when to use Hard Blue, etc.

If you've mastered all the techniques I have listed above, and if you understand the variables of waxing, you should be in good shape to select a wax.

Read the labels. That's what I do.

Funny thing, but I've outwaxed more coaches than you can imagine by simply following the directions on the wax tins. Most foreign companies have full-time waxing experts who are continually testing their products. These fellows really know their stuff and the only problem for us in North America is that sometimes something will get lost in a faulty translation on the tube. I recall one brand which described the snow conditions for three different klisters in the same way. That wasn't much help, but we knew the klisters were color-keyed (see below) with other companies' waxes and were able to go on from there.

TWO GOOD RULES–OF–THUMB

The most general rules I can give you are these, and if you follow them you'll be in the ball park at least 90 percent of the time:

I. LEARN HOW TO USE ONE BRAND OF WAX THOROUGHLY BEFORE BRANCHING OUT TO ANOTHER LINE.

There are at least ten good brands of waxes on the North American market these days and I dare say the vast majority of skiers could get along famously using just one of them.

Learning about one wax includes the study of the basic variables in waxing and of the refinements in application methods as well as the use of combinations. Here's a good example of a combination. During the early days of my waxing career Swix was the dominant wax. At one point the company produced Hard Blue and Hard Red, but no Purple. We often had a need for something like the Purple that was still in the future, so we mixed Blue and Red 50–50 on those occasions. We knew what this combination would do and later, when Swix manufactured Purple, we knew exactly how it too would perform.

II. ALWAYS USE HARD WAX FOR SNOW THAT IS IN ITS ORIGINAL STATE. USE KLISTERS FOR SNOW THAT HAS MELTED AND REFROZEN.

And Two Helpful Procedures

If you are choosing between two hard waxes, try the harder one —the one that is designated for colder conditions—first. If it slips too much, you can always apply the softer wax over it, even out in the snow and on the spur of the moment, *as long as your ski*

98. A waxing thermometer designed by Dan Darrow of South Newfane, Vermont, based on the "short form" type of waxing chart that used to come with each container of x–c wax.

is dry. I carry a piece of terrycloth to wipe moisture off the bottoms in cases like this.

And second: Klisters have pretty wide ranges and it's relatively easy to select one. Don't be afraid to get one that is a bit soft to begin with.

If your first klister selection is too hard, trying to add a softer klister will usually prove difficult, if not impossible. Water and dirt get into the original klister and you are apt to have a mess. In fact, it might be easier to clean up and start over again. On the other hand, if the klister is too soft it may wear off enough so that what you have left will work O.K.

COLOR–KEYED WAXES

Most brands of waxes are color-keyed. This means that the Hard Blue waxes, for instance, are all made for the same snow conditions. There may be slight differences in the Blues and if you are interested in making two of them perform the same way you'll have to make adjustments in the thickness and length of wax on the kicker strip you use.

The colors follow a definite sequence. For most companies their hard waxes go this way—from hardest to softest for snow conditions, and same sequence from cold to warm for air temperature. Special Green, Green, Blue, sometimes Special Blue, Purple, Yellow, Red. The Yellows and Reds are sometimes in different order. Some also have a binder wax which usually comes in an orange tin and is called Grundvax. I'll describe its use below.

The klisters are not exactly color-keyed according to temperatures since they overlap a great deal, but in general Red and Yellow are the softer klisters, used for warm conditions; Purple, Blue and Green are the hardest klisters, used for cold conditions, and Silver ranks somewhere between the two extremes.

About the only companies that do not color-key their waxes are the ones who specialize in having fewer waxes; say, one for cold snow, one for warm snow, and even one for in-between conditions.

PARAFFIN FOR THE GROOVE, EDGES AND TOPS

It's a good idea to try and keep purchase wax out of the grooves where it doesn't give you much extra climb, and in certain situations it could ice more easily than the wax on the running surface of your ski bottoms.

But since it's difficult to keep all the wax out of the grooves you should paraffin them after you finish waxing for climb.

Paraffin the edges and tops of the skis as well. Paraffined edges will make the skis run easier; paraffin on the tops helps protect them from moisture and, more important, keeps snow from building up on them. If you really want to carry some extra snow around as you ski, get hold of a backpack and fill it with snow, because that way the stuff won't interfere with your skis' performance.

FACTORS OUTSIDE THE WAXING ROOM

If you keep a waxing diary, making note of the snow conditions, air temperatures, and how a given wax worked on a certain day, you may run into a few discrepancies. Under seemingly equivalent conditions you will probably find that the Green you used one day worked a lot better on another day. This could be due to one or more of the conditions I list here. It is the consideration of these that separates the expert waxer from the merely good waxer.

MOISTURE CONTENT IN THE SNOW

If you pick up some snow and squeeze it in your hand every time you wax, you will begin to notice a difference in moisture content. Given the same temperature, snow on one day might be dry and on another day it might squeeze together more, or have more moisture in it.

The more moisture the snow contains the thicker the coat or the softer the wax you will need.

This snow-squeeze test is quite important when using klisters. Some granular snow that is rather cold will have a lot of moisture in it and then you should have some klister softer than Blue in your mixture—you might add Purple.

TRACK CONDITION

Let me say right here that all purchase waxes are made to perform optimally in packed snow or packed tracks. You can ski in powder snow or loose snow and get some climb from the wax, but you shouldn't expect much. You see, the theory on wax is this: When you press the ski down firmly into the track the snow crystals indent the wax surface and hold you from slipping back. When you take the pressure off the ski you can slide it ahead easily. If you don't have a firm snow surface to press the ski wax against, the crystals will not indent the wax.

Look at it this way. Sand makes for wonderful traction on the roads in winter driving conditions. It gets between your tires and the road surface and gives your tires something to grip. But how much grip does sand give when you drive around on a soft sandy beach?

So if the track you're in is soft, or loose, you'll need more kicker. Use a softer wax, or a thicker coat, or a longer kicker, or all three.

If you're skiing in new snow don't expect too much success with any wax. Actually, deep loose snow gives you hold in other ways. And I know a lot of people who would trade such snow for some purchase from wax, any day.

WEATHER FORECAST

You can be better informed about making a waxing decision if you know the weather forecast. What is the trend? If the local

Waxing

forecast calls for warming, take this fact into consideration and wax accordingly. Or, if you're going on a tour, take the next warmest wax along with you. And so on.

TRAIL EXPOSURE

If your trail is located primarily in the woods, in shady sections, or on the north slopes, you can be sure the snow will be colder than out in the open on a sunny slope. It would probably be a good idea to wax for the colder snow and take your chances with the warm stuff.

AIR TEMPERATURE *vs* SNOW TEMPERATURE

There is usually good correlation between the air temperature and the performance of the wax assigned for that temperature. For instance, if it's somewhere in the range of $-3°$ to $-8°$ C. (roughly 26° to 18° F.) outside and you have powder snow, most Hard Blue waxes will work well. But you might go out on Blue in conditions like this someday with a friend only to have him tell you he is on Hard Green wax, and really enjoying it—good purchase, good glide, the whole works. Chances are the snow temperature is considerably colder than the air temperature, thus accounting for the difference in wax performance.

If you know two things about snow temperatures it will help you wax. First, snow temperature is almost always colder than air temperature; this should be obvious on days when the air temperature is above freezing, because if snow gets above freezing it turns to water. Second, snow temperatures rise more slowly than air temperatures do.

In the case above, the "Blue wax" day was probably preceded by some colder weather which helped to make the snow cold, and it was still cold even though the air temperatures had warmed.

Cold temperatures form more small, very sharp ice crystals, or snowflakes if you want to call them that. Sharp crystals will more easily indent hard wax than the softer, more rounded crystals that make up warmer snow. So when I'm serious about waxing I whip out two thermometers, one for the air temp and one for the snow temp. If the air is $-5°$ C. (23° F.) and the snow is $-10°$ C. (14° F.) I would start testing Green, or even Special Green, and then work up from there, knowing I could easily add a softer wax if it was needed.

MIXING KLISTERS

You can mix klisters in the pot or on the ski. I've already explained the pot method; it's amazing what you can get away with. I've seldom made a serious error when brewing klisters, and my success may be due to the wide range of temperature conditions that most klisters work in.

If you don't want to mix up a batch of klister in a pot, or if you like certain kinds of art work, don't hesitate to mix the wax right on your ski. Putting on a few strips of Yellow, Red, and Silver and then scraping them in together leaves a lovely, colored design on your skis. That's worth something right there! (This particular color combination might work well for variable, wet granular conditions, by the way.)

I've mixed about one part Purple to three or four Blue for conditions that looked like straight Blue; this is a favorite.

Silver is a good toughener and I've mixed this successfully with all the other klisters. It makes the mixture last longer and often will provide extra speed.

Silver is the most magical wax I know. I've even used it alone, thin, for old, cold, hard-packed powder snow. Explain that one by reading the labels!

HARD WAX OVER KLISTER

This is technically one of the toughest wax jobs to put on your skis. But it's theoretically one of the easiest mixtures to understand. One set of conditions which lends itself to this combination is a hard granular track with some newer powder snow blowing in and around it. If you were to wax for the granular snow alone (with klister) it would be slow as death in the powder; if you waxed for the powder alone (with hard wax) it would soon wear off in the granular. So you compromise, and use both klister and hard wax. If it was fairly cold you could put on some Blue Klister in the usual manner and set the skis outside to allow the wax to freeze. Then, while outside, put a hard wax like Blue or Green over the klister. If you have a delicate touch you can carefully cork the hard wax without getting it

Waxing

thoroughly mixed in with the klister. Then the hard wax will carry you through the powder snow and the klister will work for you in the granular sections of the track.

The expert waxer will know just how hard to cork the wax and just how much of the klister to "pull through." Success depends on several factors, such as the condition of the track, the state of the newer powder snow, the temperature trends, etc.

The general rule for combining klister and hard wax is this: If the track dictates using a particular kind of klister and it begins to snow, or there is some loose snow blowing around, use the appropriate klister for the granular snow, freeze it, then cover it with the appropriate hard wax for the powder.

Klister used this way provides a cushion for the granular snow crystals to indent. The cushion idea comes next.

Cushion Waxing

Anytime you use hard wax over klister you are applying the cushion theory. Snow crystals that might not normally indent the hard wax enough to provide purchase, will indent that cushion of klister and provide hold.

Many skiers have modified cushion waxing to the extent of using only hard waxes, and the new fiberglass skis, being rather stiff, seem to be well suited for this type of treatment. Imagine a powder-snow day, warming in the sun and staying fairly cool in the woods and on the north slopes. By using a cushion like Hard Red and covering it with something like Special Blue Hard you avoid the risk of icing in the colder snow, yet you have that cushion for the soft stuff in the sun.

Thumbnail Waxing Summary

Learn one brand of wax thoroughly before turning to another. Most tourskiers can enjoy x–c without investing in the racers' repertory of waxes anyway.

Begin waxing with a warm, dry ski in a warm room.

Choose a wax by (a) using the outside air temperature as a guide, then (b) paying attention to the range/instructions printed on each wax container's label.

Smooth the wax well, and allow it to cool outside before using your skis.

What It Boils Down To   123

Don't be afraid to experiment. Don't be bound by such statements as "'You can never put a harder wax over a softer wax": of course you can.

Keep an account of your waxing results, in your head or, better, in a little diary-notebook tucked in your box. The expert is the waxer who remembers combinations that succeeded in oddball conditions.

WAX BOX INGREDIENTS

To keep your waxes in good condition and handy, sooner or later you'll need a wax box. I recommend the kind of sturdy metal box used for tools or fishing tackle; size and complexity of compartments depend on how serious you are about waxing. I'm not sold on cloth bags, much: they're hard to clean, easy to puncture, and often wear out.

In the box you'll have your favorite waxes and a small slab of paraffin, then these things: Screwdriver and pliers. A paint brush, and a couple of corks—one for very hard and one for softer waxes, since you shouldn't use the same cork for both. Spare screws for your bindings and spare screws or nails for your heel-plates. Steel wool, sandpaper, and some clean rags. A scraper for the ski bottoms and one for the groove, and a file to sharpen the scraper. Some wire. Adhesive tape or straps for tying your skis together. Matches in a moisture-proof metal container. Hand-cleaner or Vaseline. Maybe a thermometer, for testing air and snow temperatures. If your box is big enough, a discarded but workable flatiron whose temperature settings you can rely on; or, if you're comfortable with using it, a small butane torch. The "short form" wax chart—if you can still find one these days—for the brand of waxes you prefer (mount it on a stiff card and cover it with clear plastic wrap used for food). And your small waxing diary, and a pencil.

10: Getting in Shape

In the early 1960's a chapter on training for the benefit of the tourskier as well as for the racer had to be snuck in, so to speak, lest the grunt-and-groan connotation of the word "training" make the average x–c'er feel guilty, or even spook the newcomer away from the sport.

But no longer, glory be. Today physical fitness has become an "in" thing, a way of life, for more people all the time. No longer do motorists nearly drive off the road if they see someone out running. It's O.K. to train, even seriously, because people figure you can do your thing, and they'll do theirs. What the thing is doesn't matter.

YOU'RE ALREADY DOING IT!

As a matter of fact, many tourskiers might be surprised to discover that they're engaging in activities which are considered by most coaches, mind you, as good training.

Take the tourskiers who are hiking because of a love for the woods and mountains and the out-of-doors in general. It's a natural thing for them to be out exercising during the seasons of the year when there is no snow. The lover of hiking doesn't think of himself as training when he's out on a trip in the wilderness. But any coach I know would accept this as training for his athletes.

Naturally, good rugged work around your place—like digging ditches or sawing wood—is good for you.

So no matter what your preference is for various forms of exercise, if you enjoy a certain amount of physical work as part of your lifestyle, then you have it made. You'll be healthier and happier, and you'll have a built-in training program.

Even the serious competitors enjoy hard work and the company of other athletes in their training endeavors. They look forward to long runs or bike rides with their companions and the social aspects combine with the other rewards to make training a way of life.

99. They're not hiking above the timberline only because they're x–c skiers—they just like mountains.

Train the Way You Ski

First and most important: If you're in your middle years, you ought to have a check-up from your doctor before you embark on any sort of training program. If you're a student or younger, you should be under the supervision of a coach. Therefore I'll assume that you have had a medical examination by your family doctor or your school doctor.

This commonsensical statement now made, I'll offer another piece of advice: When you train, use the same effort you'll ski with.

For instance, if you approach tourskiing like walking, and don't like training *per se*, just forget about "training." Who ever heard of training for walking? Walking is its own training, and you just go at it. Well, you can also do your x–c this way.

If you want to step up a notch and condition yourself for some longer tours of 10 to 15 km, or if you want to train for a tour race so you can give your special rival a good run for his money, then here are several factors you should take into consideration—even if you train only a few times a month.

Training should be varied and enjoyable, challenging, measurable and progressive.

100. Change-of-pace and challenge: keys to any training program.

VARIETY AND ENJOYMENT

This is fairly obvious. If your training becomes boring, soon you won't enjoy it. I believe that people who go out and do the same bit of exercise daily have a lot of persistence—more than I have, certainly—and that if they varied their program they would be better off physically as well as mentally.

You don't have to run, run, run all year. You don't have to bike, hike, jog or lift weights continuously either.

Vary it. If whatever you're doing begins to get dull, or isn't fun any more, change something. Do something different, go out with different people, take some time off. Don't be afraid to have some fun in your training. Almost anything goes as long as it's good exercise.

THE CHALLENGE

If your training has a bit of challenge to it, you'll ultimately feel the rewards for having done it. I don't think it's much to go out and do something that's real easy and doesn't make me puff more than once or twice. My chest still swells right up, though, after I've accomplished a decent sort of workout.

Make It Fun   **127**

The challenge can take many forms. There may be a particular goal you have in mind, like running a hill on your route without stopping to walk, or biking a certain section of road in a given time, or hiking over a mountain range in so many hours. Or you might have a standard piece of work to complete in a given time. And the challenges can vary. What's right for you may be too tough or too easy for the next guy.

YOUR PROGRESS

You can measure your progress or ability to complete a self-imposed stint in many different ways. The most common method is to time yourself for the duration of a specific workout. You might occasionally run a course for time, and see how your new time compares with earlier ones.

But you can also measure yourself by how you feel. I think this is the most important measurement. Unless you're vying for a berth on the Olympic track team, no one expects you to run a sub-4-minute mile, so if you happen to be running a mile for fitness' sake it's not important to time yourself. See how you feel after it's done. If you're limber, relaxed and exhilarated, what more can you ask?

However, if you want to begin checking your progress because you're on a special program, with goals in mind, then you will probably want to time yourself once in a while. But try to steer away from the stopwatch if you're training solely for skiing.

By all means *don't set your sights too high too soon.* Make your progress slowly. Chip away at it and take your time. If your goals are attainable you'll get an extra psychological boost. Too many people go on crash programs and try to improve too fast, only to suffer setbacks, get discouraged—and quit.

THAT BUILT–IN CONTROL

Fortunately, when most people exercise too hard they don't feel exactly on top of the world and so they slow down. If you are training you should at least use that feeling of discomfort as a warning signal. If you experience pain anywhere, slow down or stop whatever you're doing. Rest for a day or two, or more; and next time out try something less rugged.

I've been told that some young people with strong hearts can work or exercise themselves to the point of exhaustion, or until some part of the body stops functioning properly—like legs not responding to efforts to make them move—and do not do themselves any harm in this process. I've never seen a situation like this and really don't want to. I don't think that you, either, should expect your legs, say, to stop moving when you are near the point of overtaxing yourself.

THE CARDIOVASCULAR SYSTEM

Most of the training for distance events like x–c races is concentrated on improving the cardiovascular system—that is, developing an athlete's ability to pump or deliver oxygen in the blood to all parts of the body. There is a great deal of debate over the most efficient way to train your system, and if you read enough of the literature you can find almost any theory you like. But there's one thing for sure: not many doctors, at least in the United States, have studied very much about training for x–c skiing. There are lots of articles written about distance events in track, but few on skiing. (Realizing this, a few years ago I came out with my special book primarily for the x–c racer, subtitled *Training and Technique for the Serious Skier.*)

Skiing as a distance event is so relatively new in this country that few physiologists have focused on it. Because of the lack of information on x–c training many coaches err in relating training for skiing with training for the running events in track. In x–c skiing, though, the upper-body muscles of the back, shoulders and arms come into play much more than they do in straight foot-running. Many believe that a slight build in the upper body is an advantage for track; on the other hand, if you didn't have enough strength in your upper body for x–c you'd be finished.

Then too, running an x–c race is a series of extremely high-effort periods interspersed with other periods of rest when you go downhill. This is different from the rest a competitor gets in running on a circular track, which he doesn't get until the race is over; and even the rest a cross-country foot-racer gets on downhill sections isn't all peaches and cream.

TRAINING ROUNDUP FOR TOURSKIERS

I'd like to list some basic training workouts, but first let me finish

101. Hill-bounding with poles is a tough one that will take anybody down a peg or two.

summarizing my theories on your training (assuming you aren't headed for the Olympics).

1. If engaging in activities considered "training" is a way of life for you, you will be in good shape and will never have to worry about a formal program to get in better condition.

2. All-round body strength is necessary for x–c skiing. The best way to condition yourself for x–c skiing is to ski cross-country. That should be obvious. But during the off-season if you are thinking about your training, do something for your legs, arms, shoulders and back. You'll find specific ski-oriented exercises described in a minute.

3. The best-conditioned people in the world are the ones who have a good cardiovascular system. Bulging muscles are not an indication of this. You can't discount the fellow who is carrying around something that looks like a beer belly either. Dr. Kenneth H. Cooper's books on Aerobics treat this subject quite well.

GOOD TRAINING COMPONENTS

Serious skiers group their training in different categories. A well-rounded program contains workouts from each category almost every week during the year. Many athletes even train twice a

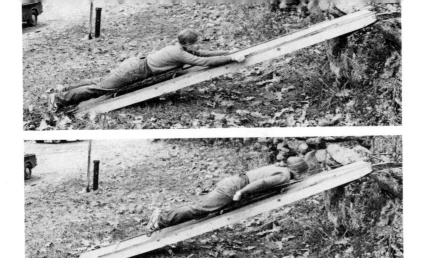

102 and 103. Time spent on the roller board builds arm strength for double-poling.

day, five to six days a week throughout the year. This is the extreme in dedication. You have the Olympics in mind when you train like this.

I'll list each category and make a few comments, giving examples.

Specificity and Co–ordination Exercises

Cross-country skiing used to be one of the most underrated sports in the country as far as physical demands were concerned. If you still think x–c can't be a real workout, just jump in the track behind an FIS or Olympic skier and see how you fare. (A friend who didn't know any better told me once that all there was to x–c skiing was "getting your wind and a little bit of stride." I almost jumped down his throat.)

A recent trend in ski training has been toward ski-oriented or specificity exercises. Roller-skiing heads the list since it is so similar to x–c on snow. Other exercises include hill-running with poles, and the use of armbands or a roller board to simulate the poling motions. There is little doubt that these exercises are some of the best you can do and that they will help your conditioning and your technique.

But remember: *If all other factors like training, strength, wax, etc., are equal, the skier with the best technique is going to be the fastest.*

Roller–skiing

Skiers in our area have been at roller-skiing for many years, dating from the mid '60's. We've seen the models change time after time and the pattern has been a familiar one. Some of the first roller skis were real klunkers and I wonder how we managed them at all. Then a few companies came in with some rather makeshift equipment that didn't work well or last long, and now —due to increasing popularity—several companies are beginning to vie for leadership in the production of roller skis.

The main virtue of roller-skiing is that it is very much like snow skiing. The movements are exactly the same although perhaps not so quick as on snow. Roller-skiing is an excellent way to train, to practice technique, and to get around on the roads. It's thrilling—sometimes a bit too thrilling!—and no doubt will continue to increase in popularity.

SOME DRAWBACKS IN ROLLER–SKIING

There are several drawbacks to roller-skiing and with its increased use by tourskiers I quickly point them out:

1. If you are not a good snow skier you may have trouble with the roller skis and fall. When you fall it's awfully tough landing on the pavement.

2. Road and highway traffic is always a threat to pedestrians, so if you go out of control on roller skis the results could be very serious.

3. Due to the danger, many areas, and some countries, are outlawing the use of roller skis on public highways. You might get a pair of skis and find you couldn't use them in your area anymore, so inquire.

It follows that when you begin roller-skiing you should select a road that is not heavily traveled.

If the downhills are at all steep you are well advised to take your skis off and walk rather than risking a fall or collision.

Practice just a few minutes a day for several outings until you gain some skill and balance. Then you can take longer trips.

Getting in Shape

104. Ski-striding at top speed makes a good specificity exercise for the diagonal. Below (105), the Norwegian version of armbands is a good rig for developing diagonal poling.

106–108. Another spot of specificity. Various types of roller skis at top. In 107 (middle), Swiss Coach Uli Wenger checks out 1975 U.S. Team members—left to right, Tim Caldwell, Chris Haines and Bill Koch—as they get ready for a 50–km spin on Vermont highways. And, bottom, how they looked in transit behind Uli's pacing bike.

I think we will soon find roller skis that are designed for use on smooth terrain like athletic fields, golf courses, etc. This will take the skiers off the highways and offer a more pleasant outing in general.

Some firms have already designed special tracks which can be laid out on gentle terrain and used for roller-skiing. These are quite expensive and have not caught on yet here in North America.

Other companies are working on some less expensive tracks, or strips, which can be laid on the ground and used with real skis of the waxless variety. One track I have tested works well with mohair skis. You might watch for something like this.

I feel that any training you can do in other sports, and especially any coaching you can get in other sports during the off-season, is going to help you with your co-ordination and therefore help you with your x–c technique. These are all good: playing different games like softball, soccer, tennis, or doing tumbling and trampoline work, or diving. I once even had instruction in modern dance for members of the U.S. Team, and it was well received.

Distance (Endurance) Training

This is just what it says: a long workout that's designed to build endurance in the athlete. A rough guide for the time of the workout is twice the time it takes to race the event you're training for. Therefore some skiers training for the 50–km race—which takes around three hours—go out for as long as six hours at a clip.

Many physiologists, coaches and trainers feel that distance training is the most important aspect of any athlete's program.

Running, jogging, biking, hiking in rugged terrain or with a pack, canoeing, kayaking, rather heavy work like logging or pick-and-shovel jobs—all these qualify as methods of endurance training. Another rough guide is this: Your heartbeat should average right around 120 per minute, counting spurts and lags, during these workouts.

Furthermore, it probably makes sense to take it easier for at least one day between good (for "good," read "hard") distance days. The body can use the respite to recover.

Training Components   **135**

Interval Training

Interval training is repeated exercises broken up by "rest" periods.

The most common type of interval training is running. Athletes run a prescribed distance at a fixed speed, return to the start and rest, or jog a bit until they are rested, and run again. There are lots of variables here—the number of intervals you do, the distance you run, the speed with which you run, and the amount of time you rest. For instance, the number of repetitions might vary from 5 to 50, the distance from 50 yards to several hundred yards, the speed at which you run from half-effort to all-out, and the degree of rest from partial to fairly complete.

Here are a couple of rough guides to help you with your interval training.

Rest after each set until your heart rate goes down to 120 per minute (I'm assuming you worked hard enough to get it up over 120). Get a rough approximation of the recovery time you need to get your pulse back down. Continue with the exercises until your recovery time is quite a bit longer than it was at first, or until you feel tired or stiff doing your workout. If doing an interval workout seems to take too long—i.e., that it takes too long to get tired or to slow down your recovery rate—then you can work harder or longer at your particular exercise. For instance, you might be running 60–yard intervals and find it takes a long time to get the effect of having had a workout. So jump the distance to 80 to 100 yards and run faster.

One theory behind interval training is that while you are waiting for your heart rate to return to 120 you are actually conditioning your cardiovascular system because of the stress it is under. Herein lies the beauty of interval training. During a period of 20 minutes of interval training, you might actually be resting or jogging, while your recovery takes place, for 12 to 14 minutes. In other words, your leg muscles, etc., are not being called upon to perform under stress for more than 6 to 8 minutes.

Proponents of the interval-training method claim that in addition to being a good conditioner for the cardiovascular system, it at the same time improves your ability to recover from vigorous exercise.

You can do lots of things for interval training. The more common approaches are running, biking, swimming or rowing

109. Getting ready to charge a hill on a three-state training trip.

rather vigorously for short periods of time. But, during a distance workout, you could incorporate some interval training by going fast for a stretch and then taking it easy (like jogging while running, coasting while biking or skiing, etc.) for a while until your recovery was complete.

Speed/Tempo Training

This kind of training is interpreted two ways. Generally, tempo training means training at racing speed, for whatever event you are working for. Speed training can mean this also; but it is used by some to mean sprint, or top-speed, training. I shall use it as meaning sprinting or going all-out.

TEMPO TRAINING

Tempo training is used to condition yourself for performing at racing speeds. It is so similar to interval training that often the two kinds of workouts are lumped together. Sometimes tempo training takes place for periods of time equal to 1/3 to 2/3 of the time required to run the event you're training for.

SPEED TRAINING

Speed training is used to train the body to be able to perform faster.

Training Components

With speed training, by my definition, you go all-out for a rather short period of time, then take a good rest by waiting until the pulse is well under 120 per minute, and repeat.

Strength Training

Most of the recent advances and changes in the training program of top athletes have occurred in their strength-training program. Almost every world class athlete does some kind of strength or weight training these days.

If you have access to some weights, or some of the more sophisticated equipment like Universal Gyms and the Nautilus machines, you can work out a very good program for yourself. But be sure to do it with the advice of someone competent in this area. There's no sense in straining or injuring yourself through ignorance.

I count three kinds of physical strength. One is gained by weight-lifting, which is especially good for those muscles involved in lifting weights—and these are not always the same ones that you need in skiing.

Another kind of strength is gained by doing special exercises related to the skiing motions, like pulling on tough elastic ropes or similar devices that offer resistance when you pull. (A couple of decades ago we were using old bicycle innertubes for such exercise; they became known as "Putney armbands.")

The third kind of strength training is that which develops what I call over-all co-ordinated body strength. When you get out there skiing you have to put it all together. The fellow who can press a lot of weight or pull the armbands until the cows come home is not necessarily going to be able to combine all his movements into a strong, co-ordinated effort on the ski track. Certain kinds of exercises like rock-climbing and gymnastics are very good for this co-ordinated strength.

Other hard work like shoveling, digging ditches (without a backhoe), cutting wood with an axe, chain-saw (these are O.K.) or cross-cut, all qualify. Hiking with heavy packs is good.

Summarizing: The best training programs contain a good balance, without short-cutting any phase. Don't think that, if you practice technique to make up for lack of training, you'll make it in a race: you'll get too tired.

Training on Snow

Often you can combine some ski training with some technique work. For instance, as you do certain kinds of interval training you can also practice flat or uphill technique. So, most of the exercises listed below will help your technique as well as improve your conditioning.

ON THE FLATS

1. Follow a good skier, stride for stride, so that only a foot or so separates the rear of his ski and the front of yours. This way you can see the power of his stride and get a good workout as well.

2. Make parallel tracks and ski beside another person. If you are a teacher this is a good way to observe where the faults and excellences are. As a skier, you can also get a good feel for how the other fellow is doing.

3. Follow-the-leader is always fun, especially if you switch the lead often. Hard-packed or granular snow is usually most suitable for this.

4. We've spent lots of time mimicking other skiers, especially well-known international ones. This is a form of technique training in that you try for a special effect or style in your skiing by copying someone.

We've had fun imitating the general styles of the Scandinavians. Several Norwegians ski with a straightforward, classic style, and these skiers are good to copy. And then there are others who have quirks—like the Swedes, who often ski very vigorously, but not too smoothly. But the favorite of all is Walter Demel, the German, who agitates so much as he skis around the track that we call him "The Human Bendix." Washing machine or not, he has sure won his share of races.

UPHILL

Since about half the time during a tour, or race, is spent skiing up hills, it's a good idea to spend about half your time on uphill training. Anyone can practice the different techniques very easily if he has a hill that is fairly flat at first, then gets gradually steeper until he's forced to resort to a herringbone to get to the top.

SHIFTING GEARS

Coaches, or teachers, can stand on the side of the hill and observe how well their skiers handle each situation: flat-skiing technique on the gradual uphill, hill-running on the steeper sections, and the herringbone on the steepest section. Some skiers will shift gears earlier than others.

In addition, it's always interesting to time the skiers as they use different techniques, thus to determine the fastest method of getting up a hill.

EFFORT AFTER THE CLIMB

Lots of skiers die out once they reach the top of a hill. After some practice it's worth continuing your uphill effort across the top and perhaps another hundred meters, or at least to the next downhill section. Two skiers might have the same time up a hill, but one could gain several seconds on the other because of a continued effort at the top.

DOWNHILL

In addition to ideas prompted by Chapter 6, Technique, you can:

1. Find a downhill section with a straight outrun and take turns coasting down it. The person who can coast out the farthest has the best downhill crouch and/or the best wax. You'll be surprised at the difference here.

2. Set up easy slalom courses and ski or race them. Or set up slalom courses on the flat and race them. This is a good double-poling practice.

3. Find a good downhill section, open, and have freestyle championships to see who comes down with the most *élan*. Powder-snow conditions are ideal for this. You'll need an impartial judge, what with all the hoopla.

A FEW POLING EXERCISES

Look again at the Technique chapter. Then:

1. Double-pole across a flat section, or a slight incline, up or down, using no strides. Keep skis together.

2. Double-pole using just one step for each poling action. Use the same foot for a while, then shift and use the other foot; continue, alternating the lead foot.

3. Single-pole across a flat using no steps or strides.

4. Single-pole up a slight hill, again using no strides.

AFTER THE WORKOUT

After some good exercise the best thing you can do is come in and take a shower, hot bath or a sauna. Then, cool off gradually and rest awhile.

I noticed that the top Russian athletes all take long rests of several hours after their distance events. They feel this is the best way for the body to recover to a normal state.

Lots of skiers wonder what to drink after sweating profusely. The current thinking espouses the importance of replacing body liquids, even during races—hence the food stations in 30– and 50–km events. For many years coaches felt a high concentration of sugar or dextrose was good to feed during and after racing or heavy exercise, but now the emphasis is on the quantity of liquid instead of the strength. You should replace what you lose through perspiration.

The popular drinks like Sportade and Gatorade are not loaded with energy, but rather have minerals like salt in them which replace those body minerals lost through sweating. It may sound crazy to you that an athlete would gulp down a salt-flavored drink during a race, but many do it and it seems to work fine.

DIET

If you have a good appetite and a well-balanced diet, there is no need to alter anything in order to go touring vigorously. You'll just find that after a day out in the country your appetite will increase. Eat up. You've earned the extra food.

Many athletes use a system called *carbohydrate loading* before an important race. One regime calls for going out about three or four days before the event and taking a hard workout, thereby depleting the body's stores of blood sugars. Then for the days

110. Boris Sapronenkov, genial physician for the Soviet X–C Team, stands by with a choice of drinks at a food station during the 1972 Olympics at Sapporo.

remaining before the race, a diet consisting mainly of carbohydrates is used. The theory is that the body builds up extra stores of energy this way.

There are various other methods for "carbo loading" but these are advised only for the top racer, who has been exposed to them during his months of hard training.

I know that the Russian skiers have had roast chicken before their races. Most coaches and athletes will tell you that you shouldn't eat anything during the three hours preceding a race and what you eat before then should be rather light at that. Well, chicken an hour and a half before a race doesn't qualify for that theory. I'll take the Russian results, though—along with their diet!

11: Where to Find It

"Anywhere there is snow cover" is the answer x–c'ers are likely to give when you ask where skiing can be found. And they're right. But there are a few considerations worth mentioning, such as whether you want to go alone, perhaps breaking out tracks; or would like to try one of the x–c areas that are mushrooming over North America; or might want to join friends to go on a citizens' race, or even take in an event sanctioned for official points in national rankings.

Therefore I present the different sorts of outings in two sections. The first offers some ideas for going x–c alone or for exploring. The second discusses organized x–c areas and mentions groups where you can get information or skiing, or both.

Out on Your Own

Right in Town

Even though you live in a city or a large town you'll be amazed at how a few imaginative questions can turn up places to go junketing x–c. Call up the municipal recreation and parks departments: maybe they don't yet have x–c trails *per se* but what about jogging and biking paths? Lacking these, are there any places *not* to ski on, like spots with special plantings?

In minimal snow cover, investigate the local athletic grounds. Many a ski training session has taken place on football or soccer fields.

Canada has pioneered with municipal x–c complexes, and right in my own back yard, so to speak, there is excellent skiing in Ottawa, and in Ste-Anne-de-Beaupré and Québec City. And I know plenty of skiers who have toured up and down the Cambridge shore of the Charles River (Massachusetts), or buzzed around the Boston Common or through New York's Central Park.

111. Author's wife on a triple-track trail during a trip to Germany. (You'll note that her waxer missed it again!)

In the Suburbs

In the suburbs there are even more possibilities. Golf courses are ideal for an undemanding tour; they're also a good place to stretch out and practice at top speed.

Again, the local rec department can tell you of hiking and biking paths or riding trails. The township road commissioner is a good person to ask about unplowed back roads; so, on a larger scale, is the county highway department—which often can supply a map, to boot.

IT BELONGS TO SOMEBODY

In this chapter and the following one, Going Out for All Day, recurs the advice to get permission before you ski on land not your own. This of course holds true for golf courses, farmland, woodlots, etc.—all land not publicly owned; but often in areas owned by town, county or state there exist for the general good some restrictions on how the land can be used.

So ask. In addition to being a routine civility, asking permission indicates that x–c'ers are responsible people. It's good for the sport.

112. Snow is where you find it on a late spring junket on the north mowing.

And in the Country

Then you get into the country and here truly, with proper permissions, x–c is anywhere there's a few inches of snow.

If you're new to a locale but want to do some exploring, go to a village and ask around for some hints. Don't overlook the proprietors of crossroads gas stations, or the fellows who plow the roads.

If you want a definite route you can usually get an old map; especially since America's Bicentennial, most towns have historic maps of some sort. Or a geodetic survey map will have old roads and trails marked on it. Many hiking trails are good. If you have used them during the summer you'll know the terrain.

Some power-line swaths are easily navigated.

Naturally, anywhere you see those familiar x–c tracks, you have a lead. Abandoned railroad rights-of-way, certainly on the increase these days, are also good.

More Organized

There are literally hundreds of places you can go if you're looking for some other skiers or established touring trails. I can do no more than make some general suggestions since a listing would fill another book and would be continually changing anyway. But you can make up your own local guide with a bit of research.

Finding the Right X–C Area

The best places to go, without question, are areas that specialize in ski touring. The good ones have everything from soup to nuts for the x–c skier.

There are three criteria you should look for in selecting an area whose specialty is x–c. First, there should be a daily instruction program, one which gets the beginner far enough along so that he can deal with a tour of his choice. Second, the area should have regularly maintained trails of varying length and difficulty, well marked, and swept at the end of each day. Third, it should have plenty of good rental equipment, along with waxing facilities.

In addition, there are many Alpine resorts that have good Nordic skiing programs staffed by good instructors.

PLAIN TALK ABOUT INSTRUCTION

There's been criticism of instruction for tourskiers: either that (1) it is provided at all; or (2) that it puts a tyro out on the trails that overtax his abilities, thus leaving him with a distaste for x–c; or (3) that it exposes beginners to expert technique.

On the first point, if you don't believe in instruction that's O.K. You don't have to succumb, but can do it your own way.

However, at this writing there are probably 1,000 certified ski-touring instructors in the United States alone. Most of these teachers belong to professional organizations that are continually studying the best methods of instruction, among other things. They care, they want to help you to become a happy x–c'er. You might give your local group a try some day.

The second point really should be refuted. True, many x–c areas are being staffed by former coaches or racers, a number of them Olympians. But the implication that naturally those nasty old racers and coaches are perpetrating a hurry-up-and-get-out-there-like-a-hotshot approach just ain't so. No, it's the less experienced x–c teachers, or the new riders on the x–c bandwagon, who are very often the ones who are trying to make beginners progress too fast. The coaches and racers I know well have been skiing x–c for years, and they're still in the sport because they love it, and so they know the ins and outs of how to get other people to enjoy it too.

As for the point on teaching expert technique—well, there are racing techniques and there are racing techniques. I have pointed out that modern racing is undergoing changes and I think what we used to consider racing technique "in the olden days" will now become accepted as expert touring technique, and that the racers will possess a style of their own for a long time. My definition of expert touring technique is that which is the most efficient way to ski. It's the technique where you get the most for your effort. It's the optimum way to ski. That's the way I try to ski, even when I'm "racing."

A good area should have a trail system complete with markings, and a map showing difficult trails, vertical climbs and drops, etc. The trail-sweep at the end of the day is an important consideration. No matter what, a skier can sometimes get lost or have equipment trouble, and if he is out late in the afternoon the trail-sweep will pick him up. In my conversations with area managers they remark that the trail-sweep is worthwhile even if only one straggler is picked up all season.

RENTALS (AND WAXING)

You don't have to rely solely on the x–c area for rental service but most such places are set up for it, and the chances are that you will have better luck if you go with them all the way. You know how it is when you take your new GM car to a Ford dealership for servicing . . .

In any case, you shouldn't have to get hung up on waxing. If you use the waxless skis you are all set, at least temporarily. If the place rents you skis, it obviously has wax, benches, and all the other facilities for waxing, and you can let them do it for you.

TRACKS vs NO TRACKS

Before I discuss the value of tracks I want to mention the gen-

Checklist of Services   147

eral difference between touring terrain in the eastern part of North America and in the West. Snow in the East is likely to be harder and, further, terrain in our mountains is choppier—more rugged and with more undergrowth—than prevails in, say, high country in the West. Like all generalities, this one of course has plenty of exceptions, but it does account for a good deal of the controversy on this side of the Atlantic over the pleasures of packed trails with tracks as opposed to no packing and no tracks.

Tourskiers of long standing always remember with pleasure some of their super days out on the snow. And depending on what section of the country they are from they will vouch for track skiing or just plain open skiing. I've been lucky enough to do plenty of both and I will admit that going out in the right conditions and skiing anywhere without having to follow a track is unbeatable. Since x–c tracks usually provide the best and most available skiing in my area, however, I follow them for 90 percent of my skiing.

The advantages and disadvantages of both kinds of skiing are pretty obvious. It may turn out that if you are in trackless ski country you will yearn for tracks and if you're in my area where tracks abound you will wait for the day when conditions permit some free skiing.

It's pretty clear that beginners can learn to ski much easier on a packed trail that has tracks set in it. The tracks help stabilize the skis, and in fact do much to direct the skis.

In general, tracks provide more uniform snow conditions and are faster. If you ski in unbroken snow you are apt to push warmer, wetter surface snow into contact with drier snow underneath, with the result that your skis ice up. You only have to compare skiing in a track to know that the track is faster. Many is the time I've leaped out of the track on a downhill to get into some unbroken stuff and slow down.

SKIING WITH A FRIEND

I'm predicting the gain in popularity of skiing side-by-side with a friend as one of the waves of the future in x–c skiing. It's easy to do in parallel tracks and you can go at your own speed and converse, if you want to. It's just like taking a walk with a buddy.

This skiing with a friend got its push from the racing scene where many courses have parallel tracks set on wide trails. Racers touring the course find it much friendlier to ski side-by-side than one behind the other. They can talk wax, technique, strategy, etc. But once they put their numbers on you won't hear much but snorts from them if they are together.

Done right, side-by-side skiing puts emphasis on the social aspects of the sport. You don't get out there and strain in pain. Instead, you get into rhythm, relax, enjoy the scenery and a conversation, and glide along in near effortless fashion. What a way to go!

BUT HERE'S THE IDEAL: CLUBS

The best is on the way, and the wonder is that it has taken so long. It's the club system, which flourishes so notably in Scandinavia, and it is beginning to catch on here in North America. The clubs promise almost unlimited possibilities for furthering all aspects of x–c, since a love of outdoor exercise is about the only credential one need have to become a member (and actually some hiking and biking groups turn to x–c in the winter as a compatible environmental sport).

Club Activities

Each club should have its own library of reference materials, including maps of all local terrain that is skiable. Various committees put on equipment sales or exchanges at the start of the season; plan social and fund-raising functions, membership drives, etc.; arrange for movies and instruction in x–c, and the latest on waxing; and organize tour races and interclub "race" races.

During the off-season there can be trail-clearing days, hikes over proposed touring terrain, plus a program of asking landowners for permission to use their properties (an established, reliable group is more likely than is an individual to be given such permission).

And finally, the grandest of all events, the big tour, can be wonderfully organized by a club. As an example, the Nordic Ski Club of Anchorage, Alaska, rents a train to get its members to the site of one of its annual tours. Membership being around 1,800 at this writing, a caravan of chartered buses wouldn't be so much fun, and riding in private vehicles could get a bit cramped.

The Value of Clubs

Their Potential for Sport and Conservation

For the ultimate in trail systems we could follow the example of Norway. There they have been at it a long time, and it shows: Skiers can go for hundreds of kilometers with assurance of being on marked terrain and finding overnight accommodations in the chain of cabins run by the Norwegian Ski Federation.

We have the same potential here in North America, and I'm confident that sometime soon we'll have the opportunity to ski 60–80 kilometers on a trip in one day, or take tours lasting several days; and neither possibility will be beyond the scope of a competent skier who's been active in a good progressive club.

Another benefit that clubs can offer is to foster x–c among young people who aren't exposed to the sport in school or college. Further, they can provide a base for x–c among those who, although they have had it in their curriculum, might otherwise give it up after graduation.

And, last, there's no question that more effort must be made to control use of public lands better, and to save wilderness areas. X–C clubs can play a big role in such conservation measures—

ABOUT TOUR RACES

In my earlier books on recreational x–c I cited the name, region, length and organizer of the most widely known established open races in the U.S.A. and the Dominion, but I'm not going to do so now. Things simply change too fast. New competitions spring up (and some older ones fade); classes and distances change; race-committee people change. Instead, I'll give you below some outfits, with addresses, to write to for the latest word on meets in your area.

Meanwhile here's a bit of advice for what it's worth: If you are beginning x–c you might be happier if you held off from any competition for a while. But if you finally get the urge to go in one of the races—"just taking it easy"—don't get carried away by the competitive spirit and exert yourself to the point of discomfort. It's well and good to talk to yourself about a low-key approach, but carrying out your resolve under the stimulus of an actual race situation is another matter.

and right on the local level, as well as banded together for broader effectiveness.

WHERE TO INQUIRE

There are three fail-safe sources of information and I refer you to them. First, *The United States Ski Association* is the parent body for a host of committees which are concerned in some way with x–c. Most of the committees have divisional or regional members and you can get their names and addresses by writing the USSA at 1726 Champa Street, Denver, Colorado 80202.

I list the committees, for your information: Hut Committee, Ski Orienteering Committee, Citizen and Club Cross–Country Racing Committee, Trail Development Committee, and the Touring and Mountaineering Committee.

To find out about qualifications necessary to enter a sanctioned race write either your USSA divisional office or your divisional Cross–Country Technical Committee. You can get both addresses from the USSA.

The second fount of information, particularly for Easterners, is the *Ski Touring Council*. This outfit has been going longer than any other present x–c group and each year publishes a huge list of touring activities. Write Rudi Mattesich, Troy, Vermont 05868.

And third: Canada is similarly divided into districts each of which operates under the *Canadian Ski Association*. For information on touring or racing you can get the address for the appropriate group in your area by writing the CSA, 333 River Road, Place Vanier, Tower "A," Vanier City, Ontario K1L 8B9, Canada.

Canada has taken the lead in North America in having more complete x–c areas than the United States. A few complexes would qualify for the running of the Olympic Games with just a small amount of work. This in essence means there are a large number of wide, well-groomed trails. In the States, at this writing, Lake Placid is gearing up for the 1980 Games and no doubt will have good facilities by then.

12: Going Out for All Day

At home in Vermont we look forward to the springs when we can go out for some nice, easy, long tours on the corn snow. If the conditions are right the stone walls and most of the blowdowns are covered with snow; the woods are never more open; and you can stay on top of the snow. We usually take a leisurely start after breakfast and spend the day at it, returning home in the late afternoon. I'll hit on some of the procedures we use in this chapter. For the extended backpacking tour, especially one that involves camping in high country like the Rockies, I recommend the Sierra Club totebook *Wilderness Skiing* by Tejada–Flores and Steck. It has lots of excellent information.

HOW FAR?

The distance can vary from a few kilometers to 40 or 50, depending on the skill of the group. Just a word of caution for everyone, however: Don't try to bite off more than you can chew. It's a good rule-of-thumb to plan any tour for a distance slightly shorter than you think can be easily managed by the least proficient skier of the group (or by anyone packing a small child). If you follow this tenet you'll all be assured of completing the trip in good shape, with time to spare for unforeseen mishaps or hang-ups.

WHO CAN GO?

Never less than three, as for any other comparable trip over remote deep-country terrain.

More than ten, on the other hand, is rather a crowd, and increases the probability of having a few of the little problems that could slow down the parade.

It adds to the fun, though, to have a variety of ages. The stronger or more competent skiers can cruise back and forth, looking for the best route and tossing a good word to their slower-moving companions.

113. Tourers enjoying some early season snow in the Canadian Rockies near Banff.

The Leader

Someone has to be in charge. This person's judgment should be respected, for he is the one who might have to make a decision to turn back, or to deviate from the normal plan. Of course he should be an accomplished skier.

The leader must be familiar with the geography and the weather of the area. There's a lot of difference between a storm rolling in around the mountains of Vermont, say, and the Rockies. What holds for one area will not hold for another, and it follows that a transplanted expert skier will not necessarily make the best leader. Give consideration to the local talent.

The leader must keep aware of the condition of the skiers in his group, and gear the speed to the slowest person. On long excursions a skier can run out of blood sugar and be unable to proceed for a period of time. In foul weather there is the danger of hypothermia. Any leader should be well versed in first aid and winter survival techniques and be ready to take action in any emergency situation.

THE ROUTE

It's always a good idea for everyone to look at the planned route

Everybody's Welcome

on a map. This is educational, it provides for a certain amount of incentive, and in case anyone does get lost it might make a big difference.

If you can plan the trip to follow the sun as much as possible it will make your trip more pleasant. For instance, if there's a choice between touring around the north side of a mountain, and the south, try the south. (Unless you're in the Southern Hemisphere. Or you want to avoid some wet snow on one side.)

If your route allows the possibility of beating a hasty retreat, all the better. Sometimes the weather socks in, or the group is not making the progress it expected to, and the wisest thing to do in this event is to head back to your beginning point.

CLOTHING

I've already talked about clothing in Chapters 4 (What to Wear) and 8 (Kid Stuff), so I'll just recap here.

Many light layers are better than one or two heavy ones. Be sure the clothes breathe. Gaiters are practically a must for touring in deep-snow country.

If you're going to be out for several hours don't skimp on little items like extra hats, headbands, gloves and socks. These can easily fit in a small pack (or fannypack) and are well worth the trouble of bringing along.

If you need something bigger than a fannypack to carry your lunch and other supplies be sure it doesn't restrict the use of your arms, especially when you pole to the rear. Some packs are too wide to be used easily while touring.

One final bit of advice: Most experienced skiers try to pace themselves so as not to sweat heavily. If your clothes become soaked with perspiration you have to dry them before they will be of much use to you. The drying can be difficult, especially if it turns off much colder. So it's better to ski a little bit on the cool side, saving an extra wrap for colder weather or a long downhill run, rather than being too warm and sweating a lot.

EATING

Your food can run the gamut from a sit-down affair at a cabin in the wilderness with grilled steak, wine and the whole bit, to a few quick stops for a light snack. If the group is not in a hurry

Going Out for All Day

and can keep warm and comfortable during a lunch break, it sure is nice.

The trip should be planned so that water is available on the route; otherwise take liquids along. It has been found that liquid replacement during exercise is very important, and that in the past too many skiers have neglected this in favor of eating, or taking in nothing at all. Mouthfuls of snow, allowed to melt before swallowing, will do in a pinch if you're not really thirsty.

Here are a few old stand-bys that we've had good luck with: Triscuits and peanuts, candy such as chocolate; cheese, raisins, apricots or other dried fruit; and oranges. This all fits in a fanny-pack or a frameless backpack and is easy to carry.

CAMPFIRES

Quite a few years ago people never thought much of building a fire for lunch but nowadays the matters of conservation and pollution—not to mention consideration for the landowner, public or private—are important things to keep in mind. Therefore if you really want to have a fire you must plan ahead for it by inquiring in advance if a fire is permissible in a place you're thinking of. My home state of Vermont, being heavily wooded, requires that a fire permit be obtained from the local fire warden even though you've been given the O.K. by the institution or individual who owns the land. Statutes vary of course, so ask the fire marshal and local or state recreation and parks officials in your area what the requirements are.

And after a campfire picnic, or any pit-stop for that matter, anyone who likes unspoiled countryside enough to want to go skiing through it will leave behind only one thing: x–c tracks.

APRÈS THE OUTING

When you get back home you'll be hungry again and if you've really planned things well it will be an easy matter to put out another spread without waiting, or having one or two people feel obliged to spend an hour in food preparation.

No one in our family ever wanted to stay home just to tend the stove, so we start a soup going before we leave. Soup bones, stew meat, stewed tomatoes, celery, carrots, onions, bouillon cubes, bay leaf—and anything else left in the icebox—make a good starter. There's always some homemade bread on hand and spreads like peanut butter, cheese, jam, etc. All these dishes are easily expanded and we can handle a crowd of a dozen with aplomb.

NON–FOOD EQUIPMENT

In addition to food, someone in the group should take a few waxing and ski repair items like: A spare plastic ski tip (good for other mishaps than a broken ski); a cake of paraffin and the next softest ski wax you might need; combination knife/screwdriver; small roll of adhesive tape; matches; and a scraper.

If you're a camera bug, by all means take some pictures of your little trips. You'll get even more kick out of viewing the pictures as the years go by.

Taking overnight trips, complete with sleeping bags, tents, cooking utensils, etc., is another matter which I am not going to cover. I like camping, but in the winter I prefer to put most of my energy into skiing. However, Hurley and Osgood have written a nice book on this subject of winter camping and I refer you to it.

IDEAS FOR OTHER TRIPS

If you're part of a larger group which includes two cars, take a cross-over trip. Park the cars at opposite ends of your route, have each group meet in the middle of the tour for lunch, and proceed.

Don't forget to exchange car keys at lunch.

ORIENTEERING

Get hold of some pamphlets or the book *Orienteering for Sport and Pleasure* by Bengtsson and Atkinson, and set up a course for that.

This is a very popular sport in Scandinavia which combines map-reading and skiing skills. It's a good way to learn to read maps; and you'll need compasses for this.

You can get maps of new territory and explore it, without compasses. This is fun and it's O.K. so long as it isn't snowing so

Going Out for All Day

as to wipe out your ski tracks. I'd hate to get lost and not have tracks to follow back to my starting point.

NIGHT SKIING

Night skiing on lighted tracks is gaining here in North America and, if you get a chance, you should try it. Better yet, try to get a group together to build your own little loop, string up some carnival lights, use street lights, automobile headlights, bonfires, torches, or anything that will provide some illumination.

Once or twice a year, when there is a little powder snow on top of a good base, and the moon is full, we go out night skiing. This is some thrill!

You know those bright nights when you can see your shadow on the snow? Try it. It's quite good for your balance, since you can't see all the very small ripples in the track and you have to learn to relax and absorb the little bumps.

Finally, if you don't have a lighted track, and the moon isn't just right for you, get a headlamp of the sort miners traditionally have used and go out on your own. These are on the market now and are very handy. The lamp is light, attaches to your head with a headband, and is powered by a battery pack which you carry on your belt.

Here's one situation where you'll want to avoid a lot of bobbing of the head, or bouncing around looking from side to side. If you want to see where you're going you'll have to keep the lamp pointed directly, and steadily, ahead.

THINGS TO BE CAREFUL ABOUT

Don't get spoiled by good racing trails, or area x–c trails which are well laid out and well groomed. If you're out in the boonies, be prepared. Zinging down a hill with a carefree attitude is fine, but it can lead to difficulties. The end of a long downhill section may take you into a washout, or a fallen-in bridge, or a sharp corner that's not negotiable, or a blowdown.

BRIDGES AND BROOKS

There are all sorts of methods for crossing bridges that are in need of repair and otherwise. I can, from experience, list a few things *not* to do.

1. Don't try to use your poles on a slatted bridge, lest a point stick in between the slats and you break the pole or wrench your arm.

2. Don't try to ski directly across a bridge where your skis will get caught between loose planks or small logs. You're likely to end up with one foot sticking through, possibly down in the water. Don't ever be afraid to take off your skis and walk across or around the bridge, or the brook.

3. If there is a thin film of water at a crossing, ski through it *without* lifting your ski from the snow. If you lift the ski and then put it down again in the snow on the other side of the crossing, your skis will probably ice up—and they could stay that way for the rest of the trip.

ROAD CROSSINGS

Around our area most of the skiers have perfected the one-legged-road-crossing technique. They boom up to a road, take off one ski, and hop across the road on that free foot, carrying the other ski in their hand.

Why not take off both skis and walk across the road, as a normal person would? Good question. I guess it's quicker to do it by hopping on one foot; and anyway it's a bit of a challenge.

FENCES

Beautiful. The first skier zips across a barbed-wire fence, and disappears into the yonder. Following skiers will attack the fence in an effort to keep up. They'll get hung up on top of the strands, underneath the strands; one person will lift one strand while another farther down the line steps on it; and so on.

Saner people take their time, survey the situation, perhaps take off their skis, and get through or over the fence in the easiest manner.

Going Out for All Day

13: Putting on a "CitRace"

Tour-race organizers are becoming one of the most important fraternities in the cross-country scene. For a long time they were unheralded, taken for granted, and sometimes downright abused. But as more people learned the ins and outs of race organization and banded together, these anonymous stalwarts have become the important ones, the ones who really count at the races. This chapter is written for them.

For the benefit of do-it-yourselfers, I'll go into some detail in describing the functions of different committees that might be necessary for running a race with a field of 1,000 or more. Naturally, for smaller races you can combine work assignments.

THE ORGANIZERS

The organizers' job is to enlist a host of volunteers and then decide on such matters as the course, the field, entry fees, timing system, awards, etc. There are no definite rules for running these races, but for some good guidelines you can write to the Citizen and Club Cross–Country Racing Committee, United States Ski Association, 1726 Champa Street, Denver, Colorado 80202, or to the Canadian Ski Association, 333 River Road, Place Vanier, Tower "A," Vanier City, Ontario K1L 8B9, Canada.

On the other hand, if you want to run something more formal and important-sounding—like a National Championship or an Olympic or FIS tryout—you will have to pay strict attention to a lot of details and regulations. I am not trying to cover all these details in this chapter, because they're spelled out by the Technical Cross–Country Committee of the USSA, or by the CSA, at the addresses above.

To Find a Sponsor

One of the latest happenings in tour races is the appearance of sponsors.

There are several kinds of businesses willing to underwrite the expenses of a race in return for a bit of advertising. To mention a few: local banks, big insurance companies or corporations, manufacturers of health foods, and, in general, any company that can benefit from a healthier public.

If you have some energetic people on your organizing committee, send them out looking for a sponsor. You can offer pre-race publicity, bibs bearing the sponsor's name alongside the title of the race, results printed on the sponsor's stationery, and so on. Even a small financial cushion in the form of guarantees toward expenses can make the going much easier.

Name to this chore only those who really know the community or the outside persons being solicited, and assign the specific people to be called on.

For the Course

Some races use a loop, or trail, that begins and ends in the same place. This is like most cross-country ski races.

Some races are run from one location to another. I prefer this kind, even if only for the psychological reason of going somewhere. It's nice to be able to say, for instance, that I toured across a town line or two.

Many citizens' races use the same trail every year. This way, skiers can compare times from one year to another, and even though snow conditions are faster some years than others, it makes for an interesting addition to the race.

The length of the courses varies from a few kilometers to the real long ones—like Sweden's Vasa, which is 85 km. A standard that is popular on this continent is between 10 and 15 km. However, if you have a nifty course in mind which might go longer you shouldn't worry about it too much. Advertise the length, and any tourskier who thinks it's a bit too long should take it easy, or not enter the race. Even a course of 20 km shouldn't give the practiced tourskier much trouble if he paces himself.

For the Field

Most of the races have been open to anyone who can ski x–c over the course. I can foresee the time when some races get so crowded that they will have to be limited by age, sex, or just first-come-first-served. But right now, most entrants in the bigger races get a chance to compare their times with former Olympian and National Team members.

ENTRY FEES

We used to run our races for $1.00 per person. With inflation, added demands and complications involved in organization, those days are gone. I think it's a fair assumption that the racers should pay enough entry money to take care of any of the following expenses: printing entry blanks; secretarial help; stationery and postage necessary for sending out information, press releases, entry blanks and results; racing bibs; simple refreshments for the skiers (described later); insurance; professional help hired, such as snowplowing, policing road-crossings and parking; use of parking lots; certain maintenance work that has to be done on the trail.

I'll discuss prizes and souvenirs for finishers in a moment.

PAPER WORK AND PHONE CALLS

If you want to be barraged with letters and phone calls before a big race, just offer your name and phone number as part of the mailing address on the entry form. You'll get personal requests of every sort, and your phone won't stop ringing until days after the race is over.

Every growing race organization reaches a point where certain things have to be made impersonal for the sake of efficiency. For instance, have your entries sent to Race Secretary, c/o the address of some business, school, or club, or to a post-office box rented for the purpose (annual rent is nominal, and certainly worth the saving in peace of mind alone).

For the Trail Committee

The trail location should be determined during the off-season, well before snowtime. It should be cut and cleared—and measured, because everyone wants to know how far he skied. It is particularly important to avoid steep downhills, and all downhill sections should be followed by a straight, flat outrun. And you'll have fewer maintenance problems if the trail is out of the wind and if there aren't too many sections facing the south sun.

Ideally, the loop type of trail should be 1/3 uphill, 1/3 level and

1/3 downhill. If you are going from one location to another, though, you'll probably attract more skiers if you use a downhill route—i.e., if there's an altitude difference between the start and finish points, choose the lower ground for the finish.

After you've got the course in mind, you do what is the most important thing of all: *call in person on landowners and get their permission for the race to cross their property.* You should have insurance, and therefore be able to assure each landowner that he is not liable for damages in case of a mishap. If he wants his land used *only* for the period of the race, this fact must be made clear later on to all entrants (some of whom might otherwise want to train on the course beforehand). Of course any cutting, leveling or clearing to make a good trail must also be O.K.'d in advance.

In return, remember that it never hurts to repair fences or cut up some fireplace wood for people whose land you use. Finally, after the race is over, don't forget formal thanks.

Some shoveling or bulldozing may be necessary to smooth the trail. Sidehill sections where one ski is lower than the other are to be avoided, both from a skier's and a track-setter's standpoint.

On certain stretches you should think of how snow will weigh down tree branches hanging over the heads of skiers who are on a trail a couple of feet deep in snow. Then you'll realize that clearing limbs and brush to a height of 2 meters isn't enough. Get the tall guys in the trail-clearing group to do the high work.

After all this is done, you should place markers every kilometer along the trail and make a detailed map of the course.

RACE SECRETARIES AND DUTIES

I'm using this group as my catch-all. You'll see why when you read further. There are lots of odd jobs that can be done and, while some of them might logically fall under another special committee's function, I've chosen to put them here for emphasis.

There are the ordinary duties of getting out entry blanks, arranging for whatever prizes are decided on, accepting entries, making up the running order or assigning bib numbers, handing out numbers on the race day (and collecting them if this is necessary), keeping times and scoring results, typing up results and mailing them out—and all this is just a start. Some of the secretaries will need executive ability, or should be members from the organizing committee.

ENTRY BLANKS

How elaborate your entry form is—whether it's mimeographed or printed, and how much information it carries beyond the bare facts and regulations—depends on your budget and manpower, but here are a few ideas which I've seen used over the years.

Timing. If the blanks are mailed out too far in advance, the human tendency is to set them aside for future decision and maybe forget them altogether. If mailed too close to race time, either they come too late for many would-be entrants to make it, or the secretary is drowned in a flood of last-minute paper work. A good compromise: *mail them three weeks before the race.*

Information on the blank. Necessary are: race committee's mailing address; date, starting place, length of race; entry fee (and when/how to send it); classes; stipulations concerning early and late entries, eligibility and refunds; names of co-operating organizations or co-sponsors.

A simple map of the trail, with a profile of the course (flats, ups, downs) is almost a must. This can indicate distance and direction from nearest major highways, and locate parking and viewing areas.

Also important to mention are availability of toilets, food, waxing facilities; method of start (mass or interval); if there are shuttle buses from parking to start (if they're needed), plus any additional amenities which may be provided by the time the race starts.

RACING BIBS

Most organizers of big races use paper bibs, handing them out the day of the race and letting the competitors keep them as a memento. They cost anywhere from 40 to 60 cents and can be included as part of the entry fee. This saves the time and labor involved in collecting cloth numbers at the end of the race. A set of several hundred cloth numbers presents a real management problem when they're dirty, wet, and several are missing from the order.

PUBLISHING RESULTS

Try to get results out as soon as possible.

If the recorders have cards with all the racer information on them (prepared in advance as entries were processed, and used as described under "The Recorders," later on), and then file them according to finish order, you can have a typist start on a stencil while the race is in progress—*if it's a mass-start affair*. Even during one of these big races it's possible to get results out as the race progresses. And if you're really organized you'll have them all done shortly after the last racer finishes. It doesn't take any more time to do it this way, during the race, than it does after the race.

With an interval-start race where the competitors begin every 30 seconds, for instance, it will take longer to get out the results.

PRIZES AND AWARDS

We've never made a big deal out of prizes, sensing that the tour-skier's reward comes from doing the race rather than collecting a doodad to display in his corner cupboard. U.S. Team members who have run in our southern Vermont tour feel the same way, enjoying the carefree competition.

Since the first Washington's Birthday race here in 1963, the name of each year's over-all winner has been engraved on a permanent trophy donated by a local jeweler; the token piece of silverplate for the winner to keep was also given by friends of x–c, not bought from race funds.

Always, though, the emphasis was on an inexpensive small memento to be given each finisher—like a special little certificate mailed out after the race, officially acknowledging the skier's participation and official time. In addition, there have been modest prizes—again donated, and chosen to be useful—for class winners. These have been such things as wax, wax remover, corks, gadgets like that.

In some of the tour races in Scandinavia they use a scoring system for clubs. This can be as simple as, say, taking the first ten finishing places from each club, with the low-total group winning a rotating trophy; or, the high-score club may provide the refreshments at the next get-together.

If you can find a coach or some veteran racers who are willing to stick their necks out and prescribe wax for the competitors, it makes for a nice gesture. Lots of tourskiers admit to being in the dark about waxing and are grateful for any advice they can get.

If there are elevation changes in your course, and you want to be really flossy, you can post air temperatures, as recorded along the course, for help with waxing previous to the race. This would be most helpful for those who are waxing on their own, possibly disregarding any official waxing information given by someone in the know.

TRACK PREPARATION

The best way to prepare tracks for x–c skiing is by using a snowmobile, or some snow-compacting machine, and a track sled.

Ideally, the swath you pack should be 3 to 4 meters wide and you should have a double set of tracks. If you have a really big field you'll have to make the trail wider and set more tracks. At Vasaloppet in Sweden they set six parallel tracks for the first 50 kilometers!

The tracks themselves should be set so there is about 12 centimeters between the inside edges of each ski. If you want to get real flossy you can follow the FIS standards, which call for a distance between inside edges of 12–18 cm on the flat and 8–12 cm on the uphills. (When you ski uphill it is normal to run with the skis closer together.)

Don't bother to put tracks in around corners or on downhill turns. It is better to pack the snow well in these sections and let the skiers make their own skate-turn marks, etc.

Starting the Track

114. An all-in-one track-maker: the rigid drum packs the trail, then the sled sets the tracks.

Using the Trail Equipment

There are several hints I can give which should be helpful. In our area we have had lots of experience with snow-packing and have learned many things the hard way. The comments I make will be appropriate for machines like our snowmobiles—SkiDoos, Olympique and Alpine—and our track sled. If you have a Snocat, then you're in a different league: you can use a much bigger sled and do a better job.

First of all, be careful. Running a snowmobile can be exhausting work. Getting stuck out there in the boondocks and having to lift the machine out of deep snow, or holes, or from in between trees, is rugged. Be sure to take along a shovel and an axe whenever you go far from any roads.

Level trails. If your trail is level, it will make for easier snowmobiling. The machines aren't too effective crossways on sidehills, even when you lean out and make like an outrigger to keep them going straight up or down. In fact, if you have a lot of sidehill terrain you are in for a few thrills. During the summer we chip away at our sidehills with shovels or bulldozers, gouging skiable shelves across the faces of the hills.

Watch out for dips in the trail. It's those small ones that get you: the runners on the machine are headed uphill, the tail end is headed downhill, and the drive belt is suspended, spinning

Putting On a "CitRace"

madly. Fill the dips in. They might be ski-breakers anyway.

Pack the trail after every snowfall of six inches or so. If you wait until you have a depth of two feet of unpacked snow it will be very difficult to pack the trail, particularly the uphill sections. Most of the snowmobiles don't lack for power, as you may know, but they do need traction.

Working on uphills. There are a couple of methods we use for our uphills. If the snow is deep even after one storm, we take both vehicles out and play leapfrog. One goes uphill as far as it can without getting stuck, peels off and returns to the foot. The other vehicle follows the first's tracks and can get up farther before peeling off and coming back.

Another system is to run the course so that you can take the steep uphills going downhill, by traveling in the reverse direction.

In deep snow situations, if you can't run the course backwards as above, or take the hills the way you would like to, it often helps to foot-pack up the hill before trying it with the machine. One trip up and back will usually do the trick.

You should never pack a trail during warm weather if you know freezing weather will follow soon.

When to Put In the Track

When you pack a trail be sure not to let it set up, or freeze, too long before putting in the track. The best system is to drag the track sled right behind the machine, and pack and set the track at the same time. This may not be possible because of the snow depth or the terrain. If it isn't, do a small section of packing, then set the track. If you wait until the next day, the packed snow may be too hard. This is especially likely to happen if there is a lot of moisture in the snow.

If you have to go around a few times before setting the track, leave for the last trip the middle section where you intend to set track. Then attach the sled and set the track.

If your machine is powerful enough and the conditions are right, you can drag a skier on a towrope behind the track sled. This gives you the perfect system. It is important to ski in the tracks set by the sled soon after they're made. The tracks freeze and, if they are not skied in, many ski bindings will catch on the sides when the first skiers use the tracks later on.

If the track is set and things warm up, keep the skiers off. (It's a good idea to post the trail before the race anyway.)

If this is not possible, then here's a neat trick that will save your track. Just as the weather starts to cool, or after the skiers are done with the track, go around it with the snowmobiles and a big, heavy chain looped behind the snowmobile. The chain will wipe out the old track, or fill it in, and leave your trail looking like a new carpet. After the weather freezes you will have a loose granular condition instead of two icy ruts. Then weight the track sled if necessary and go around it again.

SETTING TRACKS IN ICE

In very icy conditions race organizers would be wise to run a short loop with a well-prepared track, rather than attempt to condition a long stretch of trail. (My Western friends grin when they read about icy tracks. But when you live in the East one of the first things you learn is to deal with situations like this.)

There are many different sleds for use in icy conditions, and most of them operate on the harrow principle. They are heavy and have a bunch of sharp, cutting edges that stick down into the crust and cut it up.

We've even used bulldozers to crush the crust.

THE TIMERS

You need someone with a cool head here to take over the timing crew. We've had good luck with math teachers in our neck of the woods, or local businessmen who know their numbers.

Various Timing Methods

The honor system. The racer shows at the start, logs in his starting time and, on completion of the course, logs in his finish time. If the course has different start and finish points, the timers must synchronize some watches; or start the race and hightail it to the finish before any racers show up. Or you could start the race by radio or telephone if this is convenient.

An electric timer. Complete with electric eye and a punch-out tape which records the times, this makes the most accurate method of timing. These timers are certainly not necessary for

115. The latest in track-sled design by Stanley Cheney.

casual tour races, but they are required for important meets like the National Championships, where many officials feel that the utmost in accuracy is necessary.

I don't want to get too much into the theory of this, but there is no accuracy advantage in using an electric timer unless you can start the race with it.

Opting for chronometer plus stopwatches. The most common method of timing these races is by using a mass start and a couple of stopwatches and a chronometer, or master clock. Ideally, you start all the racers simultaneously, using your chronometer and at least one other watch as a back-up. Then when the racers finish, record their times with the chronometer. If you want split-second accuracy, start a stopwatch on the minute, using the chronometer, when you see a racer coming into sight; stop the watch when the racer finishes, and read his time. It might be something like 27.4 seconds on your watch, and you add this to the chronometer time at which you started your stopwatch.

THE RECORDERS

The recorders are the ones who note the second a racer crosses the finish line and write it on a slip of paper, along with the racer's bib number and the minute he crossed the line.

Meanwhile, one timer has the sole job of keeping track of the minute—i.e., the minutes that the race has been in progress.

For instance, the minute-man might have said just a few seconds ago, "This is the one hundred and fiftieth minute." The second-man on the chronometer is reading, and a recorder picks up Number 87 as the runner crosses the finish line at the 46th second. The recorder writes down on a slip of paper *No. 87–150:46.*

This slip of paper is carried to more recorders who, I hope, are seated at tables in a warm room. If the race has been well organized, these recorders have a card on each racer with the following information (prepared by the secretary while processing entry blanks): name, number, club and starting time. If these cards are in sequential order it's an easy matter to pull out Number 87's card, record his finish time, make the subtraction, have it checked, and then file the card in another pile of finished racers *according to his position as a finisher.*

Now you can see one advantage of a mass start. The recorders know that everyone started at *Zero* minutes, and actually, therefore, the racer's finishing time is his elapsed race time.

However, when racers are started at 30–second or one-minute intervals, subtractions are always necessary.

There are other advantages to a mass start:

It's certainly more exciting than the standard interval start.

It's also more practical. If you have a field of 1,000 racers, it would take a long time to get them started, even at 30–second intervals.

Finally, if the watches do fail, *the order of finish after a mass start is the order of finish for the race.*

CROSS–CHECKS

Order of finish. At all races there should be at least one person who records the order of finish. Sometimes the recorders don't have the time to write down both the racers' bib numbers and the time at which they cross the finish line. If the recorder gets the seconds at which the racers cross he then can check with the person who has the numbers of the order of finish, and match them.

Back-up watches. Be sure to have back-up watches. Your chronometer might freeze or stop.

The rules for use of electric timing specify that hand watches must be used as back-ups. This makes good sense. The electric timer might malfunction. Or there might be a power failure.

FOOD STATIONS AND REFRESHMENTS

In long, official races of 30 km and over, the organizers are required to provide food stations for the competitors.

In a tour race you probably won't even need a food station. If you decide to have one, though, or if you want to serve refreshments after the race, I'll give a few popular beverages.

First, though: During a race warm liquids are easiest to swallow. Don't make them too hot. And don't serve them cold, or the racers will gag. After the race, the temperatures are the dealer's choice.

1. *A word about salt,* which often is added to compensate for excessive loss of body minerals during heavy sweating. A good test for the amount of salt to add is this: If you can just barely taste the salt in the drink after you mix it up, and it tastes a little bit bad to you, it's probably all right for the skiers who will be drinking it after vigorous exercise.

2. *Equal parts of tea and cranberry juice.* Sugar or dextrose to sweeten and salt to taste.

3. *Tea with lemon and sugar or dextrose.* Salt if desired.

4. *Gatorade, Sportade, or some equivalent.*

5. *Any sweet drink made slightly tart with lemon juice*—the extra acidity will cut phlegm build-up, called "cotton mouth." Salt if desired.

6. *Weak coffee* with sugar or dextrose.

7. "Finnish Blueberry Drink," prepared as follows: 1 can blueberries, preferably blenderized; 3 cups water; 1 cup sugar; 1 to 2 tablespoons cornstarch. Cook all ingredients except cornstarch to boiling point. Add cornstarch which has been mixed with water. Cook until mixture is thickened. Serve warm.

On the entry form the skiers should be given advance notice if there is, or isn't, going to be any food for sale after the race. If you want something more than the quenchers provided by the race committee, you might arrange with a local service club to handle the lunch.

NOTICE, TOILETS, PARKING

To be safe, you should notify all the local authorities about your race. Include the state police, the sheriff, the selectmen or town officers, the mayor—and heavens! the big politicians around the area (if you want to).

Toilet facilities, *at least* at race HQ, are a must. You know how it is. Chemical or electric toilets—those claustrophobic kiosks now prevalent at construction sites—can be rented. Look under "Toilets, portable" in the Yellow Pages.

Years ago I didn't dream that parking would be a problem at x–c races, but that day has arrived. If you figure one vehicle for every three competitors, even this number can be a sobering thought.

By having the start away from the finish you can split up the parking problem somewhat. This has been a factor in setting courses used for some tour races.

If your parking is far from the start area you can provide a shuttle service for the skiers.

OTHER SERVICES

FIRST AID

You should have first-aid provisions, as a minimum. There are plenty of skiing doctors in most x–c areas and often they will volunteer their services or put you on to someone who can cover the race. Or, representatives from a paramedic rescue team from the local fire department may donate their time—in return for a donation to their non-profit organization (this to be regarded as a legitimate race expense).

It's important to have a crew "sweep the trail" at the end of the race. Occasionally a late skier has got waylaid and needs help.

FOR THE PRESS

If you want coverage for your race you should get out some press releases before the event. If the race is big enough you'll have the press there anyway, so you should be prepared.

It's really worth having a special committee to help here. They can make desks, phones and typewriters available; be ready with interesting information on the race and the competitors; drive accredited photographers to vantage points on the course.

If press relations play a good part in your planning, you can send out with the first pre-race publicity story a mimeographed form asking the news media to indicate if they'll be sending a representative to cover the race and if the reporter will require any special help; if they want total results mailed in; if they want highlights telephoned in (collect) right after the race. Such highlights would include the over-all winner, size of the field, human-interest notes about oldest and youngest finishers, and participation by noteworthy individuals, families or clubs in their news area.

Remember that if you send out advance news releases to spark public interest in your race, you are committed to "repay" the news media by sending them results at the end of the race.

FOR THE PARTICIPANTS

Photographs. Sometimes a local professional photographer might want to set up a table in the corner of race HQ to take orders from skiers for a print of themselves in action. Aside from giving the photographer space, I don't think the organizers should get otherwise involved, especially in the matter of mailing pictures, collecting money, etc.

Results for participants. Unless getting a corrected set of final results is an automatic award for each finisher, you may want to have skiers bespeak their sets and pay a nominal fee for having them mailed home.

First-class postage on several hundred bulky envelopes can take a good bite out of the race budget. So a system that seems to work is to set up a special table on race day and assign a volunteer to sell large business envelopes to skiers for enough to cover expected postage and handling. Right then and there each skier addresses his envelope to himself, and it's filed to be stuffed and mailed when the official result sheets are ready.

THAT OUNCE OF PREVENTION

If you are in charge of a race I've found it's a good drill to sit down after you think everything is in control and let your imagination run rampant. Consider yourself in the role of many different people coming to the race. What will they be apt to want? Are you prepared?

Let's see, there are the coaches, the eager parents, the press, pregnant women, nervous grandparents, city folk driving without snow tires, young mothers looking for baby-sitters, well-meaning people who want the sport explained to them in three minutes or less, and so on.

That's not all. If you want to qualify for the ulcer fraternity, go over some of the other, more local possibilities for trouble. (These are all based on my experience and not made up, believe me.)

A landowner calls at minus 12 hours and tells you he has changed his mind about letting the course run over his property.

A soft, gentle rain begins falling on the eve of the race and you've already scraped together all the snow you can find.

The local gendarme shows in the middle of the race and asks, irately, Why all this snow across the road? (He's speaking of the precious stuff that's been hauled in and smoothed to make a track for the skiers.)

Five minutes before the race your friendly road crew comes by and sands all the road crossings.

Your supplier of tea bags discovers, just before the race, that he is out of stock.

The fellow who last used your stopwatches is (a) out of town, or (b) can't find them right now: too busy.

Then, at the Last Minute—

Your chief timer calls in sick.

Your snow-shovelers can't find shovels and come asking you for some.

Two cars park smack in the middle of a road crossing.

Spectators, eager to see the race, position themselves in the middle of the starting lane.

You prescribe some wax and then there's an eclipse of the sun.

A forerunner comes in and reports that a big tree has just blown down over the track out at the far reaches of the course, and the race is already under way.

The local dog herd engages in a free-for-all in the starting area, wiping out all the tracks and leaving mixed in with the snow lots of remains, the least of which is dog hair . . .

Well, what organizer would be without these problems? But your reward comes in knowing how much x–c skiers enjoy any sort of race. It's as simple as that.

Index

(To save space, "cross-country" is implied or abbreviated to "x–c.")